SHORT CUTS

INTRODUCTIONS TO FILM STUDIES

NEW KOREAN CINEMA

BREAKING THE WAVES

DARCY PAQUET

WALLFLOWER

LONDON and NEW YORK

A Wallflower Press Book
Published by
Columbia University Press
Publishers Since 1893
New York • Chichester, West Sussex
cup.columbia.edu

Wallflower Press® is a registered trademark of Columbia University Press

Cataloging-in-Publication Data is available from the Library of Congress

ISBN 978-1-906660-25-3 (pbk.)
ISBN 978-0-231-85012-4 (e-book)

Book and cover design: Rob Bowden Design
Cover image: *Old Boy* (2003) © Egg Films/Show East

CONTENTS

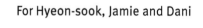

For Hyeon-sook, Jamie and Dani

ACKNOWLEDGEMENTS

Firstly, I would like to thank Kyu Hyun Kim for having helped, informed and encouraged me in so many ways over the years. Thanks also to Brian Yecies, Han Sunhee, Stephen Epstein and especially Oi Leng Lui for their comments on earlier drafts of this book. Julian Stringer gave me valuable advice in the early planning stages of this project, and I have received assistance in locating still photos from Oh Sungji and Jo Seong-min at the Korean Film Archive, Kim Heejeon at CJ Entertainment, Lim Jiyoon at FineCut, Kim Dohoon at *Cine21* and Michelle Son at M-Line Distribution. Many people have also offered their help in small but invaluable ways in the compilation of this text: Ko Yu-mi, Jang Junyoung, Abner Pastoll, Kim YeonSoo, Linda Paquet, Joseph Lim, Shin Yeo-jeong and Jeon Yoonhyung. Finally, I would like to express my gratitude to the staff at Wallflower Press, especially to Yoram Allon for his support and understanding, and to Jacqueline Downs for her careful editing of this book.

INTRODUCTION

At the opening of Park Chan-wook's *Oldboy* (*Oldeu-boi*, 2003), a middle-aged man, Oh Dae-su (Choi Min-sik) is abducted off the street and moved to a private cell where, without being given a word of explanation, he will spend the next 15 years. His suffering in this bizarre makeshift jail is partly physical (for one, he will have nothing but fried dumplings to eat over his long period of internment), but mostly mental. With a television to connect him to the outside world, he can observe the passing of time but cannot participate in it. Robbed of his freedom and the right to communicate, his very identity is threatened.

Oldboy was adapted from a Japanese *manga*, yet there is something in the situation faced by its protagonist that seems to echo the pent-up frustrations of life in pre-democratic Korea, including the challenges faced by its filmmakers. The Korean people faced a parade of nightmares in the twentieth century, from the brutal colonisation of the country by Japan (1910–45) to its arbitrary division by Western powers into mutually opposed states, North and South (1948); to the war that ravaged the peninsula and ended in stalemate (1950–53) to the political and social oppression that persisted in the postwar era and then under decades of military rule (1961–93). Life under successive authoritarian regimes involved minor and major infringements of freedom at every turn, particularly in the realm of political and artistic expression.

Throughout this period, various governments exercised control over the film industry through censorship, strict regulation of production, heavy-handed film policies, and the selective promotion of films that met their own agenda. Whether it was the Japanese colonial government banning the use of Korean language in domestic films in the 1940s, or the Park Chung Hee administration arresting director Lee Man-hee for depicting

North Koreans in too human a light in the film *Seven Women Prisoners* (*7inui yeoporo*, 1965), governments left no stone unturned in their efforts to influence the content and style of work produced by the nation's filmmakers.

Why did political leaders devote so much attention to an industry that was considered by most citizens to be merely a source of entertainment? A useful starting point to answering this question is Michael Robinson's overview of the 'political, cultural, and social obsessions' that dominated Korean life in the second half of the twentieth century (2005: 16). Political division and the traumas of war, for example, left South Korea in the position of defining itself in relation to a hostile North. As a result, the Republic of Korea became one of the most virulent anti-communist societies on earth, and any artwork or text that appeared to praise socialist ideals, or to criticise the capitalist system in the South, drew the immediate attention of the authorities. The government also encouraged a fervent nationalism in its citizens through the educational system and, indeed, through the arts, in an effort to portray South Korea as the one legitimate political and cultural system on the peninsula.

Memories of Japan's harsh colonisation also haunted Korean political and cultural life. Japan had colonised Korea in the early twentieth century with the ultimate aim of absorbing it, and particularly during the war period (1937–45) the colonial government strove to erase distinctive elements of Korean culture and encourage citizens to think of themselves as part of a Greater Japan. In the final years of the colonial period, restrictions on the use of Korean language and the forced adoption of Japanese names were widespread. After independence, Korea strove to construct a sense of Korean modernity untainted by Japanese influence, but contradictions remained. One manifestation of the country's tense relationship with Japan was a blanket ban of Japanese pop culture including films, television programmes, comic books and so on lasting all the way to the late 1990s.

The above 'obsessions' identified by Robinson relate to issues of national and cultural identity, and in this sense the medium of film came to be seen by the nation's leaders (as well as dissident intellectuals) as an important tool for influencing how the greater populace thought of themselves and their country. Until the late 1980s, the government exerted so much control over the film sector that directors with contrasting agendas were, in effect, unable to comment on the society in which they lived. A tell-

2

ing example is Lee Bong-won's mainstream youth romance film titled *What Are You Going to Do Tomorrow* (*Naeil-eun mwohalgeoni*, 1986). Produced in the run-up to the presidential elections of 1987, which had been scheduled by the government, the film included a short conversation between the two leads about future elections and the power of the electorate. Interpreting even these rather innocuous comments as anti-government in character, censors excised the scene and the film was released without it (see Park Seung Hyun 2002). Like *Oldboy*'s Oh Dae-su sitting in his cell watching television, Korean filmmakers could observe the broader changes that were sweeping through society, but could not comment on them.

Korean cinema did not win its freedom in a day, and the process of undoing the damage wrought by decades of bad policies took years. But eventually, as Korean society moved into a new democratic era, it became clear that local cinema was undergoing a remarkable transformation. Starting in the late 1980s, a group of politically and socially informed filmmakers began to explore new themes under the banner of the Korean New Wave. In the next decade, Korea's film output began to diversify in terms of subject matter, scale and genre. A new generation of directors started creating films that marked a clear break from the past and were popular with young viewers. Soon the New Korean Cinema began to attract attention internationally, both from mainstream audiences in Asia, and from festival attendees and film enthusiasts further afield. An eye-opening renaissance was underway.

At its core, the emergence of New Korean Cinema – and its precursor, the Korean New Wave – is the story of what happened when filmmakers finally escaped their confinement, and became free not only to realise a politically and socially informed cinema, but to look beyond this to an era when films were no longer obligated to speak for their nation or people. The speed and force of the transformation struck many observers as surprising, but perhaps the many years of curtailed freedoms produced in Korean filmmakers a sense of urgency and purpose that drove them forward, not unlike that of Oh Dae-su.

This book will chart the creative and commercial rebirth of Korean cinema between the 1980s and the mid-2000s, by which time the most transformative changes had run their course. Although many observers date the arrival of New Korean Cinema sometime during the 1990s – and one could begin this story with the election of Kim Young Sam as Korea's first democratically chosen civilian president in December 1992 – the roots and soul of the movement are to be found in the last decade of military rule. Any deeper understanding of contemporary Korean film classics such as *Peppermint Candy* (*Baka-satang*, 1999), *Joint Security Area* (*Gongdong-gyeongbi-guyeok JSA*, 2000) or *Memories of Murder* (*Sarinui chueok*, 2003) requires an appreciation for the demons South Korean society has wrestled in the last three decades, and how much has changed in that time. Given that many readers may not be familiar with contemporary Korean history, information on major political and social developments will be presented in this book alongside discussion of the major films and the context in which they were produced. Chapter one in particular will feature several digressions into history, which it is hoped will not only familiarise readers with some of the dramatic events that contemporary directors often reference in their films, but also give a taste of the intense and often violently confrontational nature of such incidents, which has arguably carried over into many Korean films.

Chapter one, spanning the years 1980 to 1996, traces South Korea's dramatic transformation from a highly authoritarian state into a fledgling democracy, highlighting the efforts of a new generation of socially-conscious filmmakers to advance and reflect the changing times. Chapter two (1985–96) backtracks to consider the inner workings of the Korean film industry, and the ground-up restructuring that began with the market's opening to competition from Hollywood. Chapter three traces the creative and commercial renaissance that swept the industry in the late 1990s and early 2000s, with the emergence of image-savvy, genre-inspired filmmakers who captured the attention of young audiences. Finally, chapter four considers how the successes of the 2000s led Korean directors and producers to nurture new creative and professional ambitions that would accelerate the rate of change in the industry.

The emergence of New Korean Cinema is notable in its own right, but from an outside perspective it is also a rare instance of a medium-sized national cinema growing strong enough to compete with, and even outperform, Hollywood films in its home market. Whereas many national film industries are fortunate to capture 10–15% of annual ticket sales, in the 2000s Korean cinema regularly exceeded a 50% market share, reaching a peak of 64% in 2006 (see the Korean Film Council's *Korean Cinema Yearbook* 2007). Not surprisingly, Korea came to be looked upon by neighbouring countries such as Japan and China as a model that could hold lessons for the development of their own film industries.

A short study of this sort cannot hope to give adequate treatment to the full breadth and diversity of work produced in this period, so a limited number of key films and directors will be profiled. Nonetheless, the significance of New Korean Cinema goes far beyond the names who came to attract the most fame. There is a sense of the collective about this particular film movement; of a country setting out to define itself in a new era; of decades of pent-up creative energies suddenly let loose; and of a community working together to build for the first time, after eighty years of oppression, a normally-functioning film industry.

A note to the reader: just as the term 'New German Cinema' was adopted in the 1960s and 1970s to refer to a movement that took place exclusively in West Germany, the term New Korean Cinema is used here and elsewhere to refer to films from South Korea. Unfortunately, the restricted focus of this volume will not allow for consideration of the films and filmmakers of North Korea. Throughout the period covered in this book, North Korean films were subject to completely different influences and pressures from those of the South and, due to political reasons, exchange between the two film industries was close to non-existent. For the sake of brevity, the term 'Korean cinema' will be used, but it should be understood in this context to refer to South Korean cinema.

Names and other Korean terms will be transcribed according to the Revised Romanisation of Korean adopted by the South Korean government in 2000. However, when a particular spelling has gained currency in English (for example, Park Chan-wook), or when an individual's preference has been indicated (for example, in the Korean Film Council's *Korean Film Database Book 1995–2008* (Park 2008), which collates official spellings), that form will be used. All Korean names will be written family name first in accordance with local practice.

1   A NEW SOCIETY

A middle-aged woman with a hardened, determined look on her face walks down a street crowded with protesters. She falls in among students and ordinary citizens chanting slogans and holding banners reading 'Restore Democracy' and 'Chun Doo Hwan is a Murderer'. At one point a grim silence falls when some demonstrators pull a cart filled with slain bodies through the crowd. However, her resolve to support the demonstration is mixed with rising panic: having ignored all her threats, her 15-year-old daughter has followed her from their home into the city streets. The woman implores her daughter to stay behind, but the girl, also panic-stricken, keeps disobeying and running after her. Finally they come to a large central plaza where a teeming mass of protesters have gathered, pumping their fists in the air and shouting at a formation of armed paratroopers. The soldiers are impassive, seeming to ignore them. For a few moments, the citizens' rage fills the air with an undulating roar. Then with a cracking sound, the soldiers begin firing and bodies start to fall.

This flashback sequence from Jang Sun-woo's *A Petal* (*Kkonnip*, 1996) recreates an incident that occurred on 21 May 1980 in the southwestern city of Gwangju. However, the events that set these horrific scenes in motion stretch back to the previous year and beyond. Former general Park Chung Hee had presided over Korea ever since taking power in a military *coup d'etat* in 1961. Although some Koreans now remember him fondly for the period of strong, export-led economic growth he initiated in the 1960s and 1970s, he also created a police state where the arrest and torture of dissidents, often on trumped-up charges of pro-communist activity, was common. In the 1970s in particular he had strengthened his control over South Korean society, pushing through a constitution in 1972 that granted him sweeping powers and abolished term limits on his own rule. Although he set up various legislative bodies that were made to resemble democratic institutions, with a small opposition group tolerated in the National Assembly, the system was rigged to give Park the maximum amount of power.

By 1979, however, Park was increasingly isolated and facing an unprecedented degree of resistance from the populace. A sudden economic downturn, an outbreak of labour unrest and conflict between majority and opposition lawmakers led to massive anti-government strikes in Busan and neighbouring Masan in the autumn of 1979. Then without warning on 26 October, at a private dinner party in Seoul, Park was shot and killed by his own intelligence chief and longtime associate Kim Jae-gyu.

Park's assassination was depicted in memorable fashion in Im Sang-soo's *The President's Last Bang* (*Geuttae geusaramdeul*, 2004), a work that proved to be hugely controversial even 25 years after the dictator's death. In the film, Kim is portrayed as having shot Park partly out of personal frustration, and partly out of a genuine desire to bring democracy to the country. His actions are presented as having been planned out in their broadest outlines in advance, but executed on the spur of the moment. Although this coincides with many outside views of the incident, much of that night is shrouded in mystery, and there remain questions about the true motives of Kim's actions.

The sudden assassination of such a powerful president threw the political sector into chaos. Choi Kyu Hah, who had been serving as prime minister under Park, was named acting president and promised both free elections and a new constitution. Hopes for a transition to democracy and a weakening of government authority spread quickly among the populace, though Choi's hesitant approach failed to keep pace with public demands. However, on 12 December, Major General Chun Doo Hwan, who as head of the Defence Security Command was in charge of investigating Park's assassination, staged a coup within the military. Without authorisation from Choi, Chun ordered the arrest of the ROK Army Chief of Staff and after a bloody shootout Chun and a close circle of fellow military men had gained control of the army. In the coming months he would sideline Choi and gradually take over all sectors of the government (see Robinson 2007: 139–40).

The first few months of Chun's (at this stage, unofficial) leadership were marked by confrontation. Student protests against partially-imposed martial law, which had been declared at the time of Park's death, began in earnest in March when universities opened for the new semester. Social unrest grew in April when Chun illegally took control of the intelligence agency, and culminated in a massive rally in Seoul on 15 May that drew 70,000–100,000 participants. It was Chun's draconian response to the rally that would set the stage for the violence in Gwangju.

In a show of force Chun extended full martial law over the nation, dissolved the National Assembly, closed the nation's universities and arrested 26 key opposition politicians including Gwangju hero (and future Nobel Prize laureate) Kim Dae Jung. Students in Gwangju responded with a wave of protests. A demonstration on 18 May at the gate of Jeonnam National University passed without incident; however, that afternoon as students moved to the city centre they came into contact with a group of elite black-bereted paratroopers. Sent in by the government to crush dissent, the special forces attacked students and passersby alike, in some cases using knives and bayonets. Martha Huntley, a missionary and long-term resident of Gwangju, described what she saw that day:

> One man we knew, a businessman [of] about thirty, was pulled off the bus he was riding (along with other youngish-looking people), and was kicked about the head so bad he lost an eye. Another young mother about the same age, thirty or early thirties, was taking her two children to Sunday school, was beaten and left unconscious on the sidewalk – she had to have stitches on her scalp and was incoherent for four months – her husband joined the students Sunday afternoon when they fought with the soldiers. No one knew what was happening or why. (Quoted in Oberdorfer 2001: 127–8)

The following day, as more outraged citizens joined in, the protests grew larger and more paratroopers were dispatched. Several deaths occurred. On 20 May, bus and taxi drivers went on strike and citizens began to gain control of the streets. Protesters burned government television stations KBS and MBC, as well as the tax office. On the following day, a massive rally took place in front of troops who had retreated to Provincial Hall. As depicted in the abovementioned flashback, the soldiers opened fire, killing and wounding scores of people before retreating to the edge of the city. Meanwhile, citizens ransacked rifles and carbines from local police stations and took control of the city. Over the next five days, civilian committees held negotiations with the army, as more deaths occurred on the city's outskirts. Finally talks broke down, and in the early hours of 27 May, members of the 20th Army Division moved in with tanks and put down the uprising once and for all.

The Korean press, firmly under the government's thumb, reported the uprising in Gwangju as a revolt led by communist sympathisers. The official death toll as announced by the government was 170, and a 1996 investigation raised the estimate to 240; however, many Gwangju citizens claimed the number of deaths to be higher, as many as two thousand (see Cumings 2005: 383). Authorities, meanwhile, refused to compensate victims. In the aftermath of the incident, Chun found himself firmly in power; however, news about the true nature of the uprising spread through underground sources. Later in the decade, outrage over Gwangju would serve as a key rallying point for larger anti-government protests that would prove more difficult to contain.

Filmmaking in the Fifth Republic

In the tense, oppressive years of the early 1980s, Korean cinema was doubly cursed. Filmmakers operated in an extraordinarily hostile environment due to censorship and other sorts of government interference. At the same time, the film industry had recently lost much of its leading talent. Two of the most celebrated directors of the previous decade, Lee Man-hee (*Road to Sampo*) (*Sampo ganeun gil*, 1975) and Ha Kil-jong (*March of Fools*) (*Babodeurui haengjin*, 1975), had died prematurely in 1975 and 1979, respectively. Veteran masters Yu Hyun-mok and Kim Ki-young were reaching the final stages of their career. Yu and Kim's contemporary Shin Sang-ok had mysteriously vanished in 1978, only to reappear several years later making films in North Korea with his wife, the actress Choi Eun-hee. Shin later recounted how he and Choi were kidnapped in Hong Kong and brought to Pyongyang at the request of Kim Jong Il to revitalise the industry there. After making seven feature films in the communist nation, in 1986 Shin and

Im Kwon-taek's
breakthrough film
Mandala (1981)

Choi made a dramatic escape on a promotional trip to Vienna, defecting to the US Embassy. The couple then spent several years in Hollywood, with Shin producing several films in the *Three Ninjas* series (1992–98).

Only one director who had been active during Korea's cinematic 'golden age' of the 1960s played a leading role in the 1980s and beyond, and that was Im Kwon-taek. Im debuted as a director in 1962 after serving as an assistant to director Chung Chang-hwa (who would later become famous for directing the 1972 Hong Kong film *Five Fingers of Death*). He initially found a niche as a highly prolific director of genre films, but in the 1970s his cinematic style underwent a slow evolution, as he became more interested in using the medium of film to explore the historical, cultural and artistic roots of his homeland. Neither his early genre films, nor his work of the 1970s attracted much critical attention, however.

It was only with his 75th film *Mandala* (*Mandara*, 1981) that Im would be recognised as a leading director. Based on a novel by Kim Seong-dong, the acclaimed film centres on an eccentric Buddhist monk named Ji-san who drinks heavily and remains sexually active at the same time as he pursues enlightenment through service to others, rather than meditation. The film can be seen on one level as a critique of the dominant Seon (aka 'Chan' or 'Zen') school of Buddhism practiced in Korea, which prioritises the individual's seeking of enlightenment through meditation, and encourages retreat from the concerns of the material world (see James 2002: 60). Ji-san is joined in his travels across Korea by another monk, Beob-un, and the two men's conversations form the basis of a wide-ranging debate on issues of responsibility and enlightenment.

Yet *Mandala* is just as concerned with the contemporary world as with the intricacies of Buddhist thought. Ji-san's status as a conscientious outsider who questions established doctrine contains echoes of the idealised figure of the artist, and also that of the social activist. His easy connection with the marginalised, lower-class characters who appear in the film contrasts with Beob-un's uncomfortable distance. However, Im also portrays Ji-san as being tortured by his excommunication from his faith, and the film, in contrast to the novel, ends on an uncertain note regarding Beob-un's future spiritual path.

Mandala was screened in the Panorama section of the Berlin International Film Festival in 1982, and within a few years Im would become South Korea's most familiar name on the international festival circuit. *Gilsottum* (*Gilsotteum*, 1985), about a mother, father and son separated during the Korean War and reunited in the 1980s, was shown in competition at Berlin in 1986. *Surrogate Mother* (*Ssibaji*, 1987) screened at the Venice Film Festival in 1987 and earned a Best Actress award for Kang Su-yeon – the highest-profile international accolade received by a Korean film to that date. Kang's depiction of a village girl in Joseon Dynasty-era Korea who is contracted to bear a child for an aristocratic family turned her into a major star at home, and gave her a limited degree of international recognition as well. *Surrogate Mother* would set a new export record for Korean films, with $455,000 earned in sales to Europe and Asia, and it would gross over $1 million during its commercial release in Taiwan (see the Korea Motion Picture Promotion Corporation's *Korean Cinema Yearbook* 1989: 212). In September 1988, Im's *Adada* (*Adada*, 1988) picked up another Best Actress award, this time for Shin Hye-su at the Montreal World Film Festival for playing the role of a deaf woman in 1920s Korea. Then the following year, Kang Su-yeon won yet another Best Actress award from the Moscow International Film Festival for playing a Buddhist nun in Im's *Come, Come, Come Upward* (*Aje aje bara-aje*, 1989), which explored many of the same themes as *Mandala*.

Im's films, which often combine a long-take aesthetic with emotionally direct or melodramatic plotlines, are not known for bold experiments in form. Instead, critics praise his best work for the nuanced insight he brings to the historical and cultural forces that have shaped Korea's development. Born during the Japanese colonial period in a small town outside of Gwangju, and growing up in a family accused of being leftist sympathisers,

Im describes himself as carrying on his back the 'big steel block' of history (quoted in Chung 2006: 87).

Meanwhile, other directors who were highly active during Chun Doo Hwan's 'Fifth Republic' include Lee Jang-ho, Bae Chang-ho and Lee Doo-yong. Lee Doo-yong is perhaps closest in style to Im Kwon-taek, in that his filmography spans both genre cinema and period-set dramas – though Lee's work is less didactic than Im's. *Peemak* (aka *The Hut*) (*Pimak*, 1980), which screened in competition at Venice, revolves around a female shaman who is called to a village to perform an exorcism. Possessed by spirits from the past, she uncovers a vicious crime committed by the family who summoned her. Lee's best known work *Mulleya, Mulleya* (aka *Spinning Tales of Cruelty Towards Women*) (*Mulleya, Mulleya*, 1984) was the first Korean film to screen in the 'Un Certain Regard' section at the Cannes Film Festival. Starring Won Mi-gyeong, the film details the life of a woman living in the Joseon Dynasty who is forced to marry a man who is already deceased. Lee also spent time in Hollywood, co-directing the $2 million action movie *Silent Assassins* (1988) together with his regular cinematographer Son Hyun-chae. More recently, critical interest in Lee has been revived with the screening of an uncensored version of his 154-minute epic *The Last Witness* (*Choehuui jeungin*, 1980), about Korean War-era crimes that resurface in a murder investigation decades later.

Lee Jang-ho originally made his debut in 1974 with the smash hit *Hometown of the Stars* (*Byeoldeurui gohyang*), about a woman who battles alcoholism after numerous failed relationships, but his promising career was put on hold in 1976 when he was charged with use of marijuana and banned from working in the film industry. Cleared to return in December 1979, he made an eye-catching comeback with *Fine Windy Day* (*Baram bureo joeun nal*, 1980), one of the seminal works of 1980s Korean cinema. Set in the quickly urbanising southern regions of Seoul, where people from the countryside would migrate to take up menial jobs produced by the booming economy, the film gives voice to the frustration of being passed over by Korea's rapid development. Deok-bae (Ahn Sung-ki), who delivers food for a small Chinese restaurant, develops a verbal stutter after moving to the city, and finds himself further humiliated when a rich young woman, Myung-hee (Yu Ji-in), takes up a playful, mocking flirtation with him. Chun-shik (Lee Yeong-ho), a barbershop assistant, is in love with a masseuse named Miss Yu (Kim Bo-yeon); however, she is being pursued by a wealthy loan shark who tempts her with offers to pay for her father's hospital fees. Gil-nam (Kim Seong-chan) runs errands for the owners of a 'love motel', where couples go for short trysts, but he too is betrayed and swindled. Hyangjin Lee notes that the film depicts the society of that time as 'producing essentially two types of people: one that has nothing but money to fill their empty lives, and so are always hungry for pleasure, and another that has nothing but their body to trade for survival' (2000: 170).

Of all the directors of his generation, Lee was most successful in alternating commercial hits with bold experiments in narrative and film style. *Declaration of Fools* (*Baboseoneon*, 1983) opens with a film director (played by Lee himself) committing suicide by jumping off a tall building. The film then lurches into a surreal and disjointed story about two misfits who try to kidnap a beautiful university student, only to discover that she is a prostitute. Narrated by a child's voice to a soundtrack of video game sound effects, the film's abrupt non-sequiturs and embrace of the absurd function as a strong if indirect critique of the oppressive social climate of that era. A more subdued and lyrical form of experimentation can be found in the short story adaptation *The Man With Three Coffins* (*Nageuneneun gireseodo swiji anneunda*, 1987). Told in a series of fragmented, overlapping narrative strands, the film centres around a man carrying the ashes of his dead wife to her hometown, which lies along the demilitarised zone (DMZ) separating the two Koreas. Lee uses shamanic imagery as a visual motif to create a deep and resonant depiction of Korea as a divided nation haunted by its own past.

The most commercially successful director of the 1980s was Bae Chang-ho, who received his training as an assistant director under Lee Jang-ho on *Fine Windy Day* and the heavily-censored *Children of Darkness* (*Eodumui jasikdeul*, 1981). After debuting with *People in a Slum* (*Kkobangdongne saramdeul*, 1982), an emotionally intense drama set in a Seoul shanty town, Bae turned out a string of hits which tapped strongly into the contemporary mindset. *Whale Hunting* (*Goraesanyang*, 1984) focuses on a cowardly university student, Byeong-tae (Kim Su-cheol), who embarks on a cross-country road trip with an eccentric vagabond, referred to as Captain (Ahn Sung-ki) and a prostitute, Choon-ja (Lee Mi-sook), who has lost her ability to speak. *Deep Blue Night* (*Gipgo pureun bam*, 1985), the highest grossing Korean film of the decade, stars Ahn as a Korean immigrant living in California who enters into a false marriage with a wealthy divorcee in order to receive a green card. Shot entirely on location in the US, the film paints a dark picture of the American Dream in an era when large numbers of Koreans were emigrating to America.

All four of the directors mentioned above had significant run-ins with censors in this era. A two-stage system was in place, obliging filmmakers to submit a screenplay for approval before a film went into production, and then a print after the final edit was complete. Censors had the authority to cut or re-edit films as they wished, or else to reject a film entirely if it was considered inappropriate for release. Generally, filmmakers knew better than to submit films that directly criticised the government or its policies, but even works that avoided overt political content were often re-cut by censors if they presented a picture of society that was overly dark or pessimistic. One of the most thoughtful reflections on censorship in this era is part two of Kim Hong-joon's 2003 video essay *My Korean Cinema* (*Naui hangugyeonghwa*) which in analysing the modifications made to Ha Kil-jong's *March of Fools* argues that censors had developed into skilled editors who were able to transform the mood of a sequence with just a few well-placed cuts.

There was only one area in which censorship was significantly relaxed under the Chun Doo Hwan administration. Given the deep-seated public dislike of Chun's government and general discontent among the populace, several initiatives were launched in the early 1980s to distract attention away from politics. Observers at the time sarcastically dubbed this the '3S Policy', standing for 'sex, screen and sport'. In 1982, Korea's first professional baseball league was launched. The nationwide switch to colour broadcasting also took place at this time, helping to fuel the expansion of the home entertainment market.

Finally, government censors took on a markedly more tolerant attitude towards onscreen nudity and sex, instigating a mid-decade boom in erotic feature films. The first and most famous of such works was *Madame Aema* (*Aemabuin*, 1982). Inspired by the French film *Emmanuelle* (1974), it was presented in wildly popular midnight screenings, newly legalised after the lifting of a four-decade long curfew. The story of a woman involved in numerous sexual encounters while her husband is in prison ultimately ranked as the highest grossing domestic film of 1982 with 315,738 admissions in Seoul, and would spawn eleven sequels. Although local critics found little in the film to get excited about, directors such as Lee Jang-ho

(*Between the Knees* (*Mureupgwa mureup sai*, 1984), *Eo-u-dong* (*Eoudong*, 1985)) and Lee Doo-yong (*Mulberry Tree* (*Ppong*, 1985)) would be more successful in creating innovative works within this sub-genre that also touch on issues of class and gender politics.

A new generation

At the same time that these established directors were turning out some of their best-known films, a younger generation of aspiring filmmakers was becoming engaged in the art and politics of cinema, even if they had not yet entered the mainstream film industry. Following a markedly different career path from their predecessors, this generation would, by the 1990s, play a leading role in the Korean film industry's development.

Initially, the French and German cultural centres in Seoul played an active part in the formation of this new community. With few foreign art films screened in Korean cinemas, and the country holding no international film festivals of note, it was difficult for young Koreans in the 1970s and 1980s to become acquainted with world cinema. However, in 1975 the French Cultural Centre began holding three screenings a day at its modest 119-seat theatre in Seoul, and three years later the German Cultural Centre launched a similar programme. The screenings were well attended, and before long the centres were hosting cinema clubs in which to discuss or study film (see Nohchool Park 2009). The members of this 'cultural centre generation' include many names that are now well-known, including directors Park Kwang-su (*Chilsu and Mansu* (*Chilsuwa mansu*, 1988)), Chung Ji-young (*Partisans of South Korea* (*Nambugun*, 1990)), Kim Hong-joon (*Jungle Story* (*Jeonggeul seutori*, 1996)) and Jang Kil-soo (*Silver Stallion* (*Eunmaneun oji anneunda*, 1991)); producer Shin Chul; and noted film critics Chung Sung-il, Kang Han-sub and Gina Yu.

Many aspiring filmmakers were also aligned with the broader dissident movement, which was centred in universities. Modern Korean history is steeped in a rich tradition of student protest, from the colonial period onwards. Most notably, in April 1960 demonstrations on university campuses against rigged elections grew into mass protests that toppled the corrupt authoritarian government of Syngman Rhee. Two decades later, the oppressive political situation had bred an activist movement that was increasingly displacing academics at the nation's leading schools. Many students pursued their own, parallel courses of study consisting of banned Marxist works and other political texts.

Some of the central concerns of the dissident movement are contained in the term *minjung*, a word that has acquired numerous connotations and so is difficult to translate into English. Derived from the Chinese characters 'min' (民/people) and 'jung' (衆/masses), the term can be rendered as 'the masses', but is tied to the idea of a repressed and exploited populace, the working class in particular. One of the central tenets of *minjung* theory is that the masses are the subjects, not the objects, of history, and so history should be understood from their point of view (see Standish 1994: 86). Activists felt keenly the need to establish solidarity with the working class, and thousands of students in this era left university and went to work in factories or coal mines. However, the concept of *minjung* also encompasses Korea's efforts to establish its own cultural uniqueness in the face of colonialism, war and political turmoil. Traditional Korean music and dramatic forms were embraced by students as a means of drawing closer to the nation's roots. One of the products of Korea's *minjung* youth culture was a wave of (illegal) theatrical productions that fused modern political theatre with traditional Korean mask dances, which have their own rich tradition of class criticism.

Local cinema, in contrast, was considered by many activists to be shallow and politically emasculated. However, in the late 1970s several key intellectuals, notably director Ha Kil-jong and well-known dissident poet Kim Ji-ha, began to argue forcefully on behalf of the cinema. Kim compared the works of Soviet filmmaker Sergei Eisenstein to traditional Korean theatrical genres, and encouraged artistically-minded students to explore the potential of the film medium. As interest in cinema spread, film clubs were launched in major universities in Seoul. When students began to produce their own work, they often embraced *minjung*-related themes.

By 1984, more and more amateur films and documentaries were being made on campuses and in other filmmaking groups. One prominent example was the Seoul Film Collective, launched in 1982 and made up primarily of recent graduates from Seoul National University. Including future directors Park Kwang-su, Jang Sun-woo, Hong Ki-seon, and Song Neung-han, among others, the collective produced the 8mm short *Pan-nori Arirang* (1983), which focused on an audience's response to a stage performance; *That Summer* (*Geu yeoreum*, 1984), about labourers from rural areas working in Seoul; and an 8mm documentary *Suri-se* (1984) about agricultural issues in southwestern Korea (see Gang 2005: 74–7). The group also published the influential essay collection *Towards a New Cinema (Saeroun yeonghwareul wihayeo*, 1983), which, echoing some of the ideas of the Third Cinema movement that developed in Latin America in the 1960s, called for politically relevant filmmaking that distinguished itself from both Hollywood and European art-house traditions.

Yet many of these young filmmakers faced a dilemma. The short film format offered creative freedom, but outside of informal screenings and a limited number of small film festivals, it was difficult to find an audience. The mainstream film industry offered the opportunity to reach and potentially influence many more viewers, but immense hurdles stood in the way of bringing meaningful work to the screen. Jang Sun-woo tells of his own predicament after taking on his first professional job in the film industry:

> When Lee Jang-ho made *Fine Windy Day* at the beginning of the 1980s, the political atmosphere had opened up a little, but right after that the Chun Doo Hwan regime showed its true face and the situation regressed back to that of the 1970s. At the time I was working as the script boy for Lee's next film, *They Shot the Sun* [*Geudeureun taeyangeul ssoattta*, 1981], but because the film depicted a group of social outsiders, the censors made 18 cuts to it. I was shocked, and confused about whether I should go on in the film industry. But right after that, when Lee made *Declaration of Fools*, nobody touched the film and it maintained its political message, and this gave me some encouragement. I discussed with [poet] Kim Ji-ha whether I should continue to work in cinema, and he told me it's not only a film's content that matters, he said, 'You have to change your eyes, then you can change the world.' I still remember that sentence, it was very important for me, and that's how I became interested in pursuing film style. (In Cazzaro 2005: 115–16)

A revolution, postponed

By 1987, long-suppressed frustrations were seething on university campuses, in labour circles, among the political opposition, in agricultural communities and among many ordinary middle-class citizens. Although

17

Chun Doo Hwan had taken a few steps towards reform after establishing his power – lifting martial law in 1982, and allowing his chief opponent Kim Dae Jung to return from exile in 1984 – Korea remained an authoritarian society ruled in top-down fashion. Highly-educated and increasingly wealthy after a decades-long boom in economic growth, the Korean populace was growing ever more frustrated at their lack of political representation and the general state of Korean society. Particularly reviled was the government's large and ruthless police force. Armour-clad riot cops carrying shields and clubs waged battles against student demonstrators on city streets. Plain-clothes toughs wearing jeans, helmets and leather gloves slipped into crowds and dragged off suspected activists for questioning. Young citizens accused of being communists, and threatened with jail terms or retaliation against family members, were pressured to enrol in university clubs as student spies. Meanwhile, the urban middle class had grown weary of the constant menace of tear gas, which was being used by riot cops in city centres to disperse hostile and non-hostile crowds alike.

Several incidents in the first half of 1987 served as sparks for the conflagration to follow. In January, a Seoul National University student named Park Jong-cheol died while being tortured by policemen. Interrogating him on the whereabouts of a radical student leader, the police dunked Park's head repeatedly in a tub of water and crushed his throat against the tub's rim (see Eckert 1990: 351–2). When the incident was later publicised by a Catholic priest, the government first tried to pass it off as an isolated case (even though such torture was believed to be widespread), then paid two police officers to publicly accept responsibility for the crime (see Becker 1987).

Then in April, Chun announced that negotiations on reforming the Korean constitution would be suspended until after the Seoul Summer Olympics in September 1988. This amounted to more than a mere delay, since Chun's own term expired in February 1988, and pro-democracy activists had been pushing for the next president to be chosen by popular vote.

Frustrations finally boiled over on 10 June, when former general Roh Tae Woo was named the official presidential candidate of the ruling Democratic Justice party, virtually assuring his election by the nation's electoral college. A close friend and former high school classmate of Chun's, Roh had played a key role in the military coup that brought Chun to power, as well as in the later assault on Gwangju. Students and activists responded to the announcement with the biggest wave of anti-government demonstrations since 1980. In 16 cities across the nation, protesters clashed with 120,000 soldiers and riot cops, and clearly retained the upper hand. In Seoul, conflict originally centred around Myeongdong Cathedral, where 300 students remained barricaded inside with the support of Catholic priests. In the turbulent twenty days to follow, however, more and more middle-class citizens joined in the protests, and soon all of downtown Seoul was a mass of demonstrations. Thousands of activists were arrested each day, to little effect.

Perhaps inevitably, given memories of Gwangju and the long-standing brutality of the police force, the demonstrations of June 1987 were considerably more violent in nature than those that had liberated the Philippines from Ferdinand Marcos's rule a year earlier. Students hurled rocks and Molotov cocktails at lined formations of riot cops, attacked government buildings and burned police cars. Several luxury hotels in downtown Seoul were forcibly occupied by student demonstrators. Towards the end of the three-week conflict, activists in Daejeon and Busan had taken to hijacking buses, emptying them of passengers and driving them at full speed through police barricades (see Tram & Becker 1987). Meanwhile, far from being cowed by the horrors of 1980, Gwangju provided some of the most forceful resistance of any city, with demonstrators seizing total control of the downtown area. Numerous injuries on both sides occurred throughout the conflict, although almost no actual deaths. One exception was a student from Yonsei University in Seoul who was left brain-dead after being hit in the head by a tear gas canister, but kept on life support throughout the conflict, allegedly so as not to provide another rallying point for demonstrators (see Swain 1987).

Meanwhile the twin leaders of the political opposition, Kim Dae Jung and Kim Young Sam, were alternately wooed and harassed by the government in a fruitless effort to control the crisis. Kim Dae Jung, feared by Chun for his rhetorical skills and unmatched ability to electrify a crowd, had his long-standing house arrest lifted on 24 June, reinstated eight hours later, and then lifted again the following day. In an unprecedented move, Chun also agreed to a direct meeting with Kim Young Sam, who of the two Kims was the more traditional politician. Little was achieved, however.

The government felt its hands to be tied. Day by day the situation was slipping further and further out of control, but a harsher crackdown could have disastrous implications for its image abroad. In particular, the Chun administration had planned for the 1988 Seoul Olympics to be a coming-out party: a celebration on the world stage of South Korea's economic miracle and its newly acquired status as a developed nation. Yet already the unrest was increasing the risk that the games would be shifted to another country. In one internationally reported incident, a friendly match between the Korean and Egyptian national football teams in Masan on 10 June was suspended when tear gas from a nearby demonstration wafted onto the field, causing players to stagger off the pitch vomiting (see Swain 1987). The situation called for restraint, but at the same time, Chun feared that if a democratically elected president took office in the following year, he would be tried and convicted for his role in the Gwangju massacre. Meanwhile, Chun's closest ally, the Reagan administration, was urging compromise and arguing against the reintroduction of martial law.

On 29 June, the government waved a white flag. As head of the ruling party, Roh Tae Woo issued a surprise 'eight point' reform proposal that promised a new constitution, free presidential elections by the end of the year, the restoration of civil rights to Kim Dae Jung, freedom of the press and an amnesty for most political prisoners. People power had prevailed, and Kim Dae Jung and Kim Young Sam, as heads of the opposition, seemed poised to lead South Korea into a new era.

Both Kims would eventually take their turns serving as president; however, it was not to happen in 1987. After his June announcement, Roh Tae Woo began to distance himself from Chun and issue statements in support of reform, so that many citizens began to see him as a viable presidential candidate. He also took a leading role in negotiating a new democratic constitution that was ratified by 93% of the electorate in October 1987, and which remains in place to the present day. During the run-up to the December presidential election, a strong advantage in campaign spending and biased coverage in the major state-owned television stations gave Roh an added boost. Meanwhile, despite earlier promises, the two Kims were unable to agree on an alliance before the election. With the reformist vote split, Roh won the election with 36.6% of ballots cast, compared to 28% for Kim Young Sam and 27% for Kim Dae Jung. South Korea had held a groundbreaking democratic election, but the return to civilian rule would be postponed to 1993.

The Korean New Wave

As these dramatic political developments were playing out on the streets, a group of socially conscious young directors were injecting a new vitality into the mainstream film industry. The Korean New Wave, as it was dubbed at the time by foreign critics (the term 'new realism' was initially used in Korea) was an incorporation of the *minjung* movement's focus on the exploited masses into the mainstream film industry – at least to the extent that this was possible under the existing regime. It was also a generational shift, as the students and activists who got their start in film clubs began to make feature-length work. Although perspectives on the movement vary, it would last more or less until the mid-1990s when the next generation of directors emerged.

Two developments made the Korean New Wave possible. The first was a partial relaxation of censorship, which allowed filmmakers to depict subjects and topics that had previously been off-limits. As of 1988 directors were no longer required to submit their scripts to censors at the screenplay stage, and a certain degree of social critique was newly allowed. The second was a change in film policy, discussed further in chapter two, that opened the door for independent producers to work in the film industry. This in turn made it easier for directors like the Paris-trained Park Kwang-su and the young political activist Jang Sun-woo to find like-minded producers to work with.

If there was one thing shared by the filmmakers of the Korean New Wave, it was a commitment to using the medium of film to push for social change. The turbulent political events of the late 1980s called out for a cinema that engaged with the defining issues of the day, and shed new light on Korea's troubled past. Isolde Standish describes the Korean New Wave as a shift towards 'new characters (the working classes, radical students), new settings (the factory, slum houses) and new problems (the north/south division, urbanisation, industrial unrest, and family breakdown)' (1994: 77). Kyung Hyun Kim refers to the movement as the first true flourishing of a protest cinema in Korea since the 1920s (2002: 36).

Despite the stylistic differences between the various directors, there was also a common acceptance of realism as an important aesthetic and political ideal. Decades of censorship had created a pent-up urge for a real-

Chilsu and Mansu
(1988) by Park
Kwang-su: a
pioneering work of the
Korean New Wave

ist, politically-informed cinema that put the working classes (the *minjung*) at the centre of the narrative. Although a few notable realist works such as *A Fine Windy Day, People in a Slum* and Lee Won-se's *A Small Ball Shot by a Dwarf* (*Nanjangiga ssoaollin jageungong*, 1981) had emerged in the early 1980s, the latter part of the decade marked a much more comprehensive shift. Though not for the most part popular with audiences, the New Wave represented a thematic and aesthetic revitalisation of Korean cinema.

Perhaps the most famous Korean film of the late 1980s, and one of the landmark early works of the Korean New Wave, was Park Kwang-su's debut feature *Chilsu and Mansu*. Based on a story by Taiwanese writer Huang Chunming, whose work was banned in Korea at the time, the film focuses on two billboard painters: Chil-su (Park Joong-hoon), a smooth-talker who struggles to hold down a job; and Man-su (Ahn Sung-ki), a capable and intelligent worker held back in life because he is the son of a jailed communist sympathiser. Much of the plot focuses on the frustrations they experience as marginalised members of the working class, with Man-su denied permission to work abroad and Chil-su pursuing a hopeless infatuation with a middle-class university student. They are in many ways opposites – Chil-su talks too much, and Man-su hardly at all – but they share the same alienation and sense of helplessness.

It is an extended sequence at the end of the film for which *Chilsu and Mansu* is justly famous. One hot summer day the two are atop a tall building in downtown Seoul painting a 'Glamour Whiskey' advert (featuring a smiling Caucasian woman in sunglasses and a flesh-coloured bikini) onto a giant billboard. On a break, sitting at the very top of the billboard, they drink soju and finally begin to speak honestly to each other about their failures in life. At this, Man-su stands up and begins screaming out his frustrations to all the 'well-off, educated, upper-class bastards of Seoul' living below. Chil-su joins in, and far below them a curious crowd, who cannot hear what they are saying, starts to gather. Soon, some policemen on the street hear their shouting and misinterpret it as a radical labour protest, leading to a surreal confrontation on the roof. There are multiple ironies in the way that, just when the two men finally find their voice, their words are misinterpreted and never actually heard by the people below. The state, for its part, moves in immediately to silence them. The sequence seems an appropriate symbolic starting point for the Korean New Wave, which was founded on the notion of giving voice to the oppressed, and which also had its share of confrontations with the state.

A second distinctive and innovative voice to emerge out of the Korean New Wave was Jang Sun-woo. His major films from this period include his second feature, the capitalist satire *Age of Success* (*Seonggongsidae*, 1988); working-class infidelity drama *The Lovers of Woomook-baemi* (*Umukbaemiui sarang*, 1990); his meandering critique of Korean intellectuals *Road to the Racetrack* (*Gyeongmajang ganeungil*, 1991); the Buddhist-themed *Hwa-Om-Kyung* (*Hwaeomgyeong*, aka *Passage to Buddha*, 1993); sexually explicit novel adaptation *To You, From Me* (*Neoege nareul bonaenda*, 1994); and *A Petal*, about the lingering wounds of the Gwangju massacre. All display the mark of a filmmaker who is constantly pushing into new thematic and formal territory. Jang brings an unusual psychological depth to his work, with a strong interest in sexuality and the human instinct towards violence and cruelty. Yet the actions and traits of the individuals in his films often reflect or throw light upon broader aspects of Korean society. Jang's early, realist-influenced work, *Woomook-baemi* in particular, remains much loved by Korean cinephiles and other directors to this day, but as his career progressed – and particularly with his later features *Bad Movie* (*Nappeun yeonghwa*, 1997), *Lies* (*Geojinmal*, 1999) and *Resurrection of the Little Match Girl* (*Seongnyangpari sonyeoui jaerim*, 2002) – his disorientating formal experimentation, abstract philosophical references and raw perusal of sexual themes left him an isolated figure within the larger film industry.

The Korean New Wave included numerous films that tackled social issues or depicted changes that were transforming Korean society. Park Kwang-su's second feature *Black Republic* (*Geudeuldo uricheoreom*, 1990), which many critics identify as his best work, revolves around a student activist, wanted by the police, who gets a job in a rural coal mine. Various characters in the film – the young intellectual, the blue-collar workers, the rich son of the mine owner and a prostitute who befriends the hero – reflect the fraught relations between different sectors of Korean society. Park Chong-won's *Our Twisted Hero* (*Urideurui ilgeureojin yeongung*, 1992), based on a famous novella by Yi Munyol, examines dictatorial rule on an allegorical level through the depiction of a fifth grade classroom. Several films also explore identity issues faced by Koreans who had been adopted at a young age by families in the West, including *Susan Brink's Arirang* (*Sujan beuringkeuui arirang*, 1991) by Jang Kil-soo and *Berlin Report* (*Bereullin ripoteu*, 1991) by Park Kwang-su.

Although not a single female director would debut in the late 1980s/ early 1990s, feminist issues were also taken up by male filmmakers of the New Wave. Kim Yu-jin's *Only Because You Are a Woman* (*Danji geudaega yeojaraneun iyumaneuro*, 1991) centres around a housewife who is sued after biting off the tongue of her would-be rapist. Jang Kil-soo's *Silver Stallion* depicts a woman raped by an American soldier during the Korean War, who after being ostracised by her community ends up becoming a prostitute at a US army base. Lee Hyun-seung's feature debut *The Blue in You* (*Geudaeanui beullu*, 1992) examines gender issues related to career and family, while Lee Min-yong's spirited *A Hot Roof* (*Gaegateun narui ohu*, 1995) depicts a group of women who occupy the roof of their building in rebellion against domestic violence and discrimination.

The other major category of New Wave films was reinterpretations of key events from twentieth-century Korean history. A groundbreaking work in this respect was Chung Ji-young's 1990 hit film *Partisans of South Korea* (*Nambugun*). Adapted by Jang Sun-woo from a bestselling novel, the film considers the experience of communist partisans fighting deep within Southern territory during the Korean War. Not since the 1955 classic *Piagol*, which covered similar subject matter, had a South Korean filmmaker made a film which put the audience so firmly in the perspective of communist sympathisers – although most critics consider Im Kwon-taek's later feature *The Taebaek Mountains* (*Taebaek-sanmaek*, 1994) to provide a more nuanced depiction of this sensitive historical topic. Chung also directed *White Badge* (*Hayanjeonjaeng*, 1992), an adaptation of Ahn Junghyo's acclaimed novel about South Korean soldiers serving in the Vietnam War. Park Kwang-su's *To the Starry Island* (*Geuseome gagosiptta*, 1994) centres around a massacre of civilians on a remote island by South Korean troops during the Korean War, and its lingering effect into the present day. Finally, Lee Jeong-guk's *Song of Resurrection* (*Buhwarui norae*, 1990) was one of the first mainstream Korean features to reference the massacre in Gwangju, although censors cut more than 25 minutes from the film, in addition to the 15 minutes that the filmmakers had voluntarily removed.

Conflicts with censors

The relaxation of film censorship in the late 1980s is seen as a key factor behind the development of the Korean New Wave. However, Seung Hyun Park (2002) argues that the political ambitions of Korean Wave filmmakers were still significantly hindered by the government.

Park notes that although censorship at the screenplay stage was officially discontinued in 1988, the Public Performance Ethics Committee still required producers to submit two copies of each script before the start of shooting. The PPEC would then send 'comments' to the production company, and – given the board's power to edit a film at will after its completion – filmmakers felt strong pressure to adhere to the board's suggestions. Despite this, few films passed through the final censorship stage without at least some cuts being made. According to the Sixth Revised Motion Picture Law in effect at the time, the PPEC was authorised to cut films under the following vague conditions: (1) when a film impairs the spirit of the constitution and the dignity of the state; (2) when a film impairs social order and morals; (3) when a film impairs friendship between Korea and another country; and (4) when a film impairs the soundness of the people. Government statistics indicate that only 44 of the 88 Korean films approved for screening in 1988 were passed without cuts in footage or dialogue, followed by 55 of 110 in 1989, 52 of 113 in 1990, 51 of 121 in 1991 and 45 of 96 in 1992 (see the Korea Motion Picture Promotion Corporation's *Korean Cinema Yearbook*, 1988–92).

Park points out that the board, while adopting a more flexible attitude overall, focused their energies on blocking content related to three issues:

industrial strife, oppression carried out by previous military regimes and the role of the US in Korea. His case study of Park Chong-won's debut film *Kuro Arirang* (*Guro arirang*, 1989) is a telling example. Based on a novella by Yi Munyol, the film is set in one of Seoul's infamous textile factory districts, which from the 1960s to the 1980s were witness to some of the most abusive working conditions Korea has ever known. Largely staffed by female workers from rural regions, the factories were also the sites of the country's earliest and most famous labour conflicts. *Kuro Arirang* focuses on the female worker Jong-mi (Ok So-ri) and male student Hyun-shik (Lee Kyung-young), who has joined the factory without revealing his university background in order to build solidarity between student activists and labourers. As the film progresses, conflicts arise between the workers and their manager (*Oldboy* lead actor Choi Min-sik, in his film debut) over his irresponsible conduct which has caused two lethal accidents. When workers plan a strike, the police cooperate with company bosses in order to apprehend the leaders of the action.

Park argues that given the sheer number and scale of labour conflicts in Korea during the late 1980s, *Kuro Arirang*'s content would hardly have shocked its intended audience. Nonetheless, the PPEC made 21 visual and audio cuts to the film before allowing its release (see 2002: 130). The removed elements include a scene showing a male supervisor sexually assaulting a female worker; evidence of collusion between the police and the factory management; and images of riot police trampling on a dead woman's photograph. Bits of dialogue hinting at class conflict were also removed, such as 'Rich bastard!' and the lines of a poem read by a worker. It is testament to the government's belief in the power of the film medium that, although Yi's novella was published with all these elements in place, censors considered them too incendiary to be shown in a mainstream movie.

With its most politically relevant elements excised, *Kuro Arirang* came across as disjointed and weak, with the workers appearing to lack will (the exact opposite of the filmmakers' intention). Critical response was poor, and audiences largely ignored it. Years later in 2002, a surviving portion of the deleted elements were reinserted and the film was screened on Korean public television station EBS. Nonetheless, it seems certain that the film would have occupied a far more important position in Korean film history if it had escaped the censor's hand.

Meanwhile, numerous other projects from the late 1980s were abandoned at the script stage due to the severity of PPEC comments and the like-lihood that, if the films were shot, the board would cut them beyond recogni-tion. These include Jang Sun-woo's *The Red Room (Bulgeun-bang)*, about 'a good citizen who is arrested for political activities, jailed and severely tortured' (Rayns 2007: 28), and *Samcheong Gyoyukdae*, a depiction of the infamous 1980s 're-education camps' to which the government sent crimi-nals and dissidents to engage in hard labour (see Park 2002: 127).

Roh Tae Woo's presidency and the underground movement

Roh Tae Woo was officially inaugurated in February 1988, and in certain ways Korean society began opening up to change. The country experienced an unprecedented wave of labour disputes, more or less tolerated by the government, which saw many workers receive long-overdue increases in pay. The increasing independence of the press, and a number of landmark decisions by the Constitutional Court also brought about modest but genuine expansions in citizens' basic freedoms. In the realm of diplomacy, South Korea took on a noticeably warmer attitude towards the Soviet Union, China and other communist nations; one sign of this was the first ever commercial release of films from these countries in 1988: *War and Peace* (*Voyna i mir*, 1967) and *Moscow Doesn't Believe in Tears* (*Moskva slezam ne verit*, 1980) from the Soviet Union, *When Father Was Away on Business* (*Otac na sluzbenom putu*, 1985) from Yugoslavia, and the Chinese film *The Last Empress* (*Mo dai huang hou*, 1986). Meanwhile, given the diminished powers of the presidency under the new constitution, and the dominance of opposition parties in the National Assembly, Roh's ability to set the domestic political agenda was limited.

Nonetheless an unexpected political development came in the run-up to the 1990 National Assembly elections, when Roh and opposition leader Kim Young Sam announced an alliance and merger of their two parties. Kim's supporters were stunned, but the move offered political benefits to both sides. Kim immediately established himself as the leading candidate in the 1992 presidential elections by ensuring that the government party would not field a competitor. Roh for his part acquired much more politi-cal leverage for the remainder of his term. Soon after the announcement, Roh's policies took on a more hardline bent, with an increase in political arrests and a crackdown on labour (see Robinson 2007: 170).

Meanwhile a large number of new independent film groups, often with ties to the labour movement, began to form under Roh's presidency with the aim of producing outside the mainstream industry. Although sharing many of the same goals and ideals of the Korean New Wave directors, independent filmmakers worked with considerably fewer resources and presented their works to students or workers in unofficial (and therefore illegal) on-site screenings.

The most famous of these groups was Jangsan-gotmae, named after a novel by dissident writer Hwang Suk-young. The group's first production was the 16mm feature *Oh! Land of Dreams* (*O! kkumui nara*, 1988), about a Korean student who participates in the Gwangju Uprising and is then wanted by the police. He eventually finds himself questioning his prior admiration for the United States. Shot without registering the production with the state or submitting it to censors, it was first screened in a Seoul theatre in December 1988, and went on to play before 100,000 viewers in 500 unofficial screenings across the country (see Jeong 2007: 202). In January 1989 arrest warrants were issued for Jangsan-gotmae president Hong Ki-seon and future producer Yu In-taek, who arranged for the first screening of the film.

The most famous of Jangsan-gotmae's works is the 16mm feature *Night Before the Strike* (*Paeopjeonya*, 1990), about a disagreement among factory workers which management tries to exploit on the eve of a walkout. Shot in an actual factory in Incheon which was being occupied by workers, the film features non-professional actors and was praised by Joong-Ang University professor Lee Yong-kwan for 'creating, in its content and form, a new style for national [*minjok*] cinema' (Anon. 2000: 39). Even more famous than the film itself were the circumstances surrounding its screenings. The film-makers organised a simultaneous release in eleven cities on 6 April, and the government responded by sending in squadrons of riot cops and even police helicopters. Multiple accounts tell of half an audience sitting in a darkened theatre watching the film as the other half battled riot police outside the door. Numerous arrests were made and projectors confiscated; nonetheless an estimated 300,000 people across the country eventually saw the film – the equivalent of a mainstream commercial hit (see Kim Sunah 2007a: 331–2).

Jangsan-gotmae went on to make one more film, *Opening the Closed School Gate* (*Dachin gyomuneul yeolmyeo*, 1991), before disbanding in

1993. Interestingly, members of the group included some key figures in Korean cinema's later commercial revival, including Chang Youn-hyun (director of the 1999 thriller *Tell Me Something* (*Telmisseomding*)), Lee Eun (co-president of Myung Films and producer of *JSA, The President's Last Bang*), Kong Su-chang (director of the 2004 horror film *R-Point* (*Alpointeu*)) and Hong Ki-seon (director of 2003 human rights drama *The Road Taken* (*Seontaek*)).

Another movement that was gathering steam was the emergence of independent documentaries shot on video. Kim Dong-won's *Sanggye-dong Olympics* (*Sanggyedong ollimpik*, 1987), about the forced relocation of slum residents in order to 'beautify' the city for the 1988 Olympics, is widely considered the starting point of the independent documentary movement. Inspired by the work of Japanese documentarist Ogawa Shinsuke, Kim began living among the slum residents and his filmmaking activities eventually became an integral part of their political struggle. Several years later, Kim would establish Purn Productions, which would produce 33 documentaries by various directors in the next decade and a half.

Why Has Bodhi-Dharma Left for the East?

As the Korean New Wave was struggling to take root, another important film emerged seemingly out of nowhere. *Why Has Bodhi-Dharma Left for the East?* (*Dalmaga dongjjogeuro gan kkadalgeun?*, 1989) was shot at a mountain temple in southeastern Korea by Bae Yong-kyun, a painter with a strong interest in Buddhism and Asian philosophy. Korea has produced a long line of Buddhist-themed works by such well-known directors as Shin Sang-ok, Kim Ki-young, Im Kwon-taek, Kim Soo-yong, Bae Chang-ho, Jang Sun-woo, Park Chul-soo and Kim Ki-duk. However *Bodhi* stands apart even from these in the extent to which it internalises Buddhist thought, shaping the film's own relationship to narrative and meaning (only Jang Sun-woo's 1993 feature *Hwa-Om-Kyung* comes close in this regard).

Ten years in the making, *Bodhi* centres around three Buddhist monks living in a remote hermitage: a seven-year-old boy, Hae-jin (Hwang Hae-jin), first becoming acquainted with the concept of life and death; a man in his thirties, Ki-bong (Shin Won-seop), facing an internal struggle over his decision to leave the material world – and his blind mother – behind; and the elderly master, Hye-gok (Yi Pan-yong), who offers them guidance as his own death approaches. The title is taken from a koan riddle about the Indian monk Bodhidharma who travelled eastward to China and became the first recognised patriarch of Chan (that is, Zen, or in Korean 'Seon') Buddhism. With its non-linear, image-centred narrative and cryptic dialogue, the film upsets viewer expectations to an extreme degree, like a marathon runner who turns and starts running in the opposite direction. Francisca Cho contrasts mainstream cinema, which imparts to the viewer a sense of broad intelligibility and 'mastery' over the text, with the kind of Chan discourse embraced by the film, which disrupts or undercuts any sense of a comprehensive truth or correct vision. She notes that 'Westerners who survive the pace and subverted narrative conventions of *Bodhi* will invariably want to know what it "means"', but says that is to miss the point of the film (1999: 180). She compares the work to Buddhist koans – 'speech acts specifically designed to violate and call attention to the illusion of mastery' – and argues that *Bodhi* pursues this objective by cinematic means (1999: 188).

Another major aspect of the film's achievement is its striking visuals. There is a sensuousness to Bae's images, in part because of the immense care he takes in lighting, and in part because the imagery is complemented by an unusually immediate and pure sound (though, unfortunately, there is a distracting dated quality to the post-dubbed dialogue). Natural settings, old wooden architecture, robed human figures and the occasional object from the modern world are arranged together in visual compositions that, although nearly always incorporating movement, unmistakably evoke the art of painting. On the occasions when the monks venture out into the modern world, the images are composed with equal artistry, but the chaotic, jumbled quality of the scenes comes across as a shock in comparison. Meanwhile, the music by Jin Gyu-yeong, hypnotic in its long phrasing, adds considerably to the overall atmosphere of the film.

Despite the challenges posed by the work, *Bodhi* became the first (and, at the time of writing, still the only) Korean film to win the top award at a major European festival, receiving the Golden Leopard at the 1989 Locarno International Film Festival. It also secured a $100,000 sale to France – quite significant in that Korean cinema exports in the 1980s averaged less than $300,000 per year (see the Korea Motion Picture Promotion Corporation's *Korean Cinema Yearbook* 1990). Bae would go on to make

The record-breaking
Sopyonje (1993) by Im
Kwon-taek

one more feature, *The People in White* (*Geomeuna ttange hina baekseong*, 1996), a bleak tale about memory set in an industrial wasteland, before largely retiring from public view in the following decade.

The onset of civilian rule and the Sopyonje phenomenon

As 1993 approached, a new era was dawning. Roh Tae Woo's five year term as president was scheduled to expire in February 1993, and as expected Kim Young Sam beat his rival Kim Dae Jung with 41.4% of the vote to usher in the return of civilian rule to South Korea. It was an era of new beginnings, marked by the sense that Korea was stepping out of its past and joining the community of modern nations. Kim Young Sam began his term with a 92% approval rating; his decision to purge the government of military figures and appoint intellectuals and former dissidents to key positions was broadly popular.

Meanwhile, the onset of participatory democracy caused many citizens to rethink various aspects of national identity. Over the previous three decades, Korea had gone through a stunning but highly disruptive period of economic expansion. The country had been massively urbanised. Globalisation had introduced new cultural influences into what many viewed as an ethnically homogeneous nation. Michael Robinson notes: 'A new debate emerged in the 1990s as a consequence of the rapid creation of wealth in South Korean society. How had successful economic development altered the lifestyles, but more importantly, the values of the average Korean?' (2007: 186).

As it happened, a film appeared at this time that spoke to such concerns. Im Kwon-taek's *Sopyonje (Seopyeonje,* 1993) depicts a singer of *pansori* (a kind of traditional Korean folk opera native to Korea's southern provinces) who devotes his life to teaching the art form to his adopted daughter. Set in the years after Korea's liberation from Japan in 1945, the film depicts how *pansori* falls out of favour with the spread of Western music and culture. The father Yubong (Kim Myeong-gon), his daughter Songhwa (Oh Jeong-hae) and his stepson Dongho (Kim Gyu-cheol), who has been taught to play a drum accompaniment, eke out a living by performing in street markets and at private gatherings. Soon, however, even this limited form of employment dries up. Frustrated by hunger and enraged by his stepfather's cruelty and authoritarian character, Dongho eventually runs away. Several years later, Yubong's lessons to Songhwa are taking place in isolation and poverty, and it is clear that her improving skills will bring her neither fame nor a steady income. Yet the obsessive father proves willing even to inflict shocking misfortune upon Songhwa in order to keep her at his side, and to turn her into a master.

Many observers interpreted the struggles of the family to survive as *pansori* performers as a symbol of Korean filmmakers' efforts to resist domination by Hollywood. At the same time, resting beneath the surface of the narrative is a discourse on the concept of *han* – another term that is difficult to translate into English (but which bears similarities to the Russian word *toska*). *Han* can be described as a deep-seated feeling of sorrow, bitterness or despair that originates in oppression or injustice, accumulates over time and remains unexpressed in the heart. It is believed by some to be intrinsic to the Korean cultural experience; the poet Ko Eun, for example, is quoted as saying, 'We Koreans were born from the womb of *han*, and brought up in the womb of *han*' (quoted in Yoo 1988: 222). In the latter part of *Sopyonje*, Yubong singles out Songhwa's inability to access her *han* as the one thing preventing her from achieving true mastery: 'Your *pansori* is smooth, but it lacks *han* … You have experienced more than enough pain, but your *pansori* doesn't express it.' It is only at the film's conclusion, long after Yubong's death, that the viewer knows from listening to her singing that Songhwa has tapped into this emotional reservoir.

Sopyonje was never expected to become a box-office hit. The film opened on 6 April, 1993 to a muted reception, and producer Lee Tae-won says it was almost pulled from theatres after its first week (and in many regional cities it was pulled, only to be reinstated later). However, as time passed, it soon developed through word of mouth into a popular phenomenon, with even president Kim Young Sam attending a viewing. A resurgence of interest in *pansori* followed. By October, *Sopyonje* had become the first Korean film ever to pass the one million admissions mark in Seoul, and it ended its run with 1.03 million admissions in Seoul and an estimated 2.2 million nationwide (see Kim Sunah 2007b: 339). The novel by Lee Cheong-jun on which the film was based became a bestseller, and 130,000 copies of the soundtrack CD were sold. The film was also exported to Japan, where it performed surprisingly well on limited release in 1994.

Im Kwon-taek was no stranger to box-office success – in fact, the film that *Sopyonje* surpassed to set a new local record was Im's own *The General's Son* (*Janggunui adeul*), a period gangster film that had 678,946 admissions in 1990. However, the director himself argues that had *Sopyonje* been released in the 1980s, it would not have been a commercial hit, suggesting that in some way it spoke to the needs of the moment (in Cho 2002: 150). In this sense, Songhwa's embrace of the 'uniquely' Korean emotion of *han* can be read as indicating a way forward for a culture struggling with issues of identity. Nonetheless, Im's representation of *han* is in many ways problematic. Feminist critics in particular took issue with the way that *han* and the pursuit of artistic perfection serves as justification for the violence done to Songhwa, and the implication that her suffering makes her, in some way, more authentically Korean (see, for example, Chungmoo Choi 2002).

Global ambitions for Korean cinema

Apart from the political reforms he introduced, one of President Kim Young Sam's key initiatives was to push ever more actively for the globalisation of South Korean business and society. Coined as *segyehwa* (from the roots *segye* meaning 'world' and *hwa* meaning 'becoming/turning into'), the official policy promoted broad political, economic, social and cultural restructuring, with a particular emphasis on the economy (see Shin 2005: 53). Local firms were encouraged to operate on a global scale, and to compete more effectively with international firms in the domestic market. *Segyehwa* was particularly notable for its top-down orientation (in most countries, globalisation progresses in bottom-up fashion, with government playing a supporting role), and for its ambition to affect all sectors of society. In a 1995 speech, Kim said:

> Fellow citizens: Globalisation is the shortcut which will lead us to building a first-class country in the twenty-first century. This is why I revealed my plan for globalisation and the government has concentrated all of its energy in forging ahead with it. It is aimed at realising globalisation in all sectors – politics, foreign affairs, economy, society, education, culture and sports. To this end, it is necessary to enhance our viewpoints, way of thinking, system and practices to the world class level … We have no other choice than this. (Quoted in Kim 2000: 1)

Although Korea had pursued an export-driven, internationally focused economic policy since the 1960s, Samuel S. Kim argues that *segyehwa* marked the most aggressive embrace of globalisation by any state in the post-Cold War era (2000: 2). Subsequent presidents would continue Kim's policy with similar zeal.

Meanwhile, a symbolic turning point for the film industry came in May 1994, when the Presidential Advisory Council on Science and Technology issued a videotaped report on the media sector to Kim Young Sam. Included within the presentation was the observation that in its first year on release, Steven Spielberg's *Jurassic Park* (1993) earned revenues equivalent to the export of 1.5 million Hyundai cars (see Shin 2005: 53). Given that the exports of Hyundai and other Korean car manufacturers totalled 640,000 vehicles in 1993, Spielberg's film had more than doubled the annual production of one of Korea's proudest industries. The report urged the president to support the media sector and related high-tech industries (such as computer-generated imagery) as a strategic growth sector.

Kim was convinced, and this incident can be seen as initiating a new kind of relationship between the Korean government and the film industry. Whereas in the past, film policy had been primarily geared towards regulation or control, from this point onward there was wide and unchallenged consensus that the government's primary role was to promote and support the film industry. The reference to Hyundai cars is also laced with

significance: previous governments viewed cinema chiefly as an ideologi-
cal tool, either supportive or critical of the status quo. The identification
of filmmaking as an industry that could potentially create revenues on
a par with large-scale manufacturing, however, was a significant shift in
perspective (see Jo 2005: 176–7). In the coming years, and especially
during the commercial boom of the early 2000s, more and more citizens
began to view Korean cinema as an important part of the nation's overall
economy. Jobs in the film industry became a popular choice for new business graduates. Even some of the vocabulary began to change: derogative
terms used in the past such as *banghwa* (literally 'country picture', a term
referring to Korean films) and *ttanttara* (meaning 'entertainer', a slur term
into which filmmakers were grouped) fell out of use, to be replaced with
neutral words like *yeonghwa-saneop* (film industry).

Korean films of the mid-1990s

Korean films in the mid-1990s were in a transitional phase, as the political
and social battles of the 1980s became supplanted by new concerns. This
era also saw the increased prominence of two directors who are sometimes grouped with the Korean New Wave for reasons of chronology, but
who have largely been preoccupied with different aesthetic and thematic
concerns. Park Chul-soo began his career in television in the late 1970s
before attracting notice with a series of award-winning genre films in the
mid-1980s, including *Mother (Eomi*, 1985), *Pillar of Mist (Angaegidung*,
1986) and *You My Rose Mellow (Jeopssikkot dang-sin*, 1988). However,
his most famous works appear in the mid-1990s. Park adopted a working method that contrasted with industry norms, in that he produced his
own films and kept budgets low by striving to limit the number of shooting days and making efficient use of film stock (not unlike the approach
taken by director Kim Ki-duk in the following decade). His films are known
for their focus on everyday human conflicts, presented in a freewheeling,
black comic style. He also displays a particular interest in the perspectives
and lives of women. *301,302 (Samgongil samgongi*, 1995) stars Hwang
Shin-hye and Pang Eun-jin as single women living in opposite apartments.
Song-hee (Pang) is an enthusiastic cook who, in the aftermath of a failed
marriage, turns to food for comfort, while Yoon-hee (Hwang) suffers from
anorexia after being sexually abused as a young girl by her stepfather, a

butcher. The film's garish colours and gruesome finale marked a significant departure from other realist Korean films of the time.

Farewell My Darling (*Haksaengbugunsinwi*, 1996), winner of an artistic contribution award at the Montreal World Film Festival, depicts the elaborate funeral proceedings of a family patriarch. Shifting perspectives between the various family members, who are virtually all in conflict with each other, Park satirises the family's disingenuous outbursts of grief and their stubborn adherence to complex traditional funeral rites that none of them fully know or understand. Shot in 14 days, Park's film was released in the same year as Im Kwon-taek's *Festival* (*Chukje*, 1996), which also presents a Korean funeral but in a much more reflective and reverential style.

Another director who carved out a niche for himself with a highly individual style was Lee Myung-Se. An assistant director to Bae Chang-ho for much of the 1980s, Lee made his debut in 1989 with *Gagman* (*Gaegeumaen*), an inventive comic drama about a stand-up comedian who dreams of becoming a film director. He followed that up with the commercial hit *My Love My Bride* (*Naui sarang naui sinbu*, 1990), a drama about the trials of early marriage starring Choi Jin-sil and Park Joong-hoon that would help to inspire a string of romantic comedies in the mid-1990s.

However, Lee is best characterised by his unwavering focus on what he considers the purely cinematic elements of the medium: light, movement, sound, colour. In an industry that had, for the most part, prioritised words and narrative over image, Lee's films stood out for their visual experimentation, stylish sets (often designed by the director himself) and inclination to suspend narrative development to visually depict a character's mood. *First Love* (*Cheotsarang*, 1993), which many critics consider the peak of his early career, plays with notions of cinematic time in its depiction of a university student's secret crush on her theatre instructor. *Their Last Love Affair* (*Jidokan sarang*, 1996), with actress Kang Su-yeon, depicts the slow disintegration of an extra-marital affair, with its abstract imagery imparting to the narrative a sense of finite beauty and impending sorrow.

Lee largely sidestepped the social concerns that preoccupied filmmakers of the New Wave. After the release of his critically acclaimed action/art-house film *Nowhere to Hide* (*Injeongsajeong-bolgeot eopta*, 1999), film weekly *Cine21* described Lee as 'a cinephile with a stubborn belief in his own personal creativity, and virtually the first Korean director to seriously consider fundamental aspects of the cinematic form' (Anon. 2000: 38).

In this sense, Lee should perhaps best be understood not as the black sheep of the Korean New Wave, but as a precursor of the genre-influenced, image-centred movement that took shape in the late 1990s with the debut of a new generation of filmmakers.

One other key work that emerged in the mid-1990s was Byun Young-joo's *The Murmuring* (*Najeun moksori*, 1995), the first Korean documentary ever to receive a theatrical release. The film, and two more works that followed – *Habitual Sadness* (*Najeun moksori 2*, 1997) and *My Own Breathing* (*Sumgyeol*, 1999) – detail the lives of former comfort women who were abducted by the Japanese military during World War Two and forced into prostitution. Screenings of the film in both Korea and Japan helped to publicise the women's efforts to receive an official apology from the Japanese government. Byun's interactions with the women are intimate but hands-off; although she does not conceal her presence as in works of Direct Cinema such as David and Albert Maysles' *Salesman* (1968), she tries to encourage the women to become active agents in telling their own story. By the final film in the trilogy, the women have become knowledgeable in operating the camera, and one of them acts as the film's primary interviewer.

Cinephilia blooms

By the mid-1990s a new enthusiasm for cinema was developing among Korea's youth. This may have been part of a broader developing interest in the arts: Korean commentators have referred to the 1990s as the 'decade of culture', following the 1980s 'decade of politics' (and preceding the 'decade of economics', the 2000s). But cinema held a special place in this shift, according to Soyoung Kim:

> As is often noted, the quasi-religious energy of the 1980s Korean student movement – in fact a kind of youth culture – is hardly detectable on 1990s streets and campuses. Unexpectedly, and unlike the 1980s, quasi-religious energy is found in film spectatorship. The fascination for cult movies or a mode of cult spectatorship around American B-movies, European art-house cinema, Hong Kong action movies and Wong Kar-wai, in particular, are phenomenal in Korean youth culture. The term 'cine-mania' was coined in recognition of the large number of such spectators. (2005: 82)

One of the earliest manifestations of this newly developing 'cine-mania' was an influential radio programme hosted by announcer Jeong Eun-im from 1992–95 which introduced a broad range of films to its many listeners. The year 1992 was also notable for the unexpectedly strong performance of a string of French films, including Claude Berri's *Manon des sources* (247,639 admissions in Seoul), Leos Carax's *Les Amants du Pont-Neuf* (The Lovers on the Bridge) (275,607 admissions), Marc Caro and Jean-Pierre Jeunet's *Delicatessen* (99,519 admissions), Jean-Jacques Annaud's *L'Amant* (*The Lover*) (337,233 admissions) and Régis Wargnier's *Indochine* (300,865 admissions). The surprising commercial strength of these French films, and the large number of customers requesting European art-house titles, are said to have pushed video rental shops to diversify their selections in this period (see Kim Hak-su 2002: 80–1). In May 1995, two influential film magazines made their debut: the monthly *Kino,* headed by film critic Chung Sung-il (a regular guest on Jeong's radio show), and the weekly *Cine21,* launched by Korea's leading progressive newspaper *The Hankyoreh.* Before long, *Cine21* was the bestselling weekly magazine of any type in Korea. November 1995 marked the official launch of Dongsoong Cinematheque, operated by a small art-house distribu-tion company Baekdu-daegan which was headed by future director Lee Kwang-mo (*Spring in My Hometown* (*Areumdaun sijeol,* 1998)). The video market was especially vibrant, in contrast to the 2000s, with even obscure titles finding an audience among cinephiles or B-movie enthusiasts.

What occurred in the 1990s was not an overall increase in film atten-dance – in fact, annual admissions declined throughout the decade and hit a 35-year low of 42.2 million in 1996 – but a diversification of tastes and the emergence of an influential group of cinephiles. It is not entirely unexpected that highly stylised and youthful films like Hong Kong director Wong Kar-Wai's *Fallen Angels* (*Duoluo Tianshi*) (151,163 admissions) should perform well at the box office – although its estimated Seoul theatrical take of $850,000 is almost five times its North American gross of $173,000 (see Anon. n. d.). But truly surprising was the box-office performance of several highly challenging art-house films. Andrei Tarkovsky's austere 1986 feature *The Sacrifice* (*Offret*) sold 24,743 tickets on its release in 1995 and drew a considerable amount of mainstream attention, while Iranian director Abbas Kiarostami's *Where is the Friend's Home?* (*Khane-ye doust kodjast?,* 1987) sold 48,209 tickets on a single screen release, slightly outgrossing *The Cable Guy* (1996) with Jim Carrey which was released by Columbia Tristar a month later on eight screens. Such instances led at least one Western critic to refer to Korea as 'the most cinephile country in the world' (Rayns 1996: 5). Hong Kong director Peter Ho-Sun Chan has argued that the Korean film industry's biggest strength is the sophistication of its audience (interview with author, January 2008); if true, then the origins of this are located in the cinephilia of the 1990s.

The 1990s also witnessed the birth of Korea's first major film festivals, ranging from small, independently-organised events to large-scale international showcases sponsored by metropolitan governments. Soyoung Kim argues that many of the smaller festivals that were launched in the mid-1990s, such as the Women's Film Festival in Seoul, the Seoul Queer Film and Video Festival, the Human Rights Watch Film Festival (launched by a former political prisoner) and IndieForum (organised by young independent/activist filmmakers) are extensions of the progressive movement, and a sign of its changing strategies. Particularly as the labour movement began to relinquish its position as the primary vehicle of social change in the 1990s, an increasing focus on group identities – women, gays, migrant workers, and so on – began to overshadow the 1980s emphasis on class identity (2005: 86–9). In this way film festivals emerged as a productive space in which to further define and explore these emerging identities. (For an insightful overview of such issues in relation to the 1998 Seoul Queer Film and Video Festival, see Berry 1999.)

But the most spectacular manifestation of Korean cinephilia in the 1990s was the birth of the Pusan International Film Festival (PIFF). Launched by a group of critics from Busan (spelled 'Pusan' according to the romanisation system in use at the time) together with director Park Kwang-su and former Vice Minister of Culture Kim Dong-ho, PIFF held its first event in September 1996. Organisers set a goal of selling 50,000 tickets. As it turned out, crowds of enthusiastic, primarily young viewers poured in from all corners of Korea and total attendance topped 184,000 (see Cazzaro and Paquet 2005).

In the coming decade, PIFF became arguably the top film festival in Asia, and was instrumental in helping Korean cinema build an international reputation. Successful premieres of Korean films at Pusan were often followed by invitations to European festivals like Berlin, Rotterdam or Cannes. Retrospectives of veteran filmmakers Kim Ki-young, Shin

Sang-ok, Yu Hyun-mok, Lee Man-hee and Kim Soo-yong helped to spread awareness of Korean film history. In addition, the launch of the Pusan Promotion Plan in 1998 – a 'pre-market' where Asian directors with treatments or scripts for new films are put in touch with potential financiers and co-production partners – greatly enhanced the level of interaction between Korean filmmakers and industry figures from other countries. In the coming years, two other major international festivals would emerge in the Puchon International Fantastic Film Festival (PiFan) and the Jeonju International Film Festival (JIFF). By 2007, close to forty film festivals would be officially registered with the Ministry of Culture (see the Korean Film Council's *Korean Cinema Yearbook* 2007).

Confronting the past

The 1990s were, for the most part, an era in which Korea looked towards the future. However, 1996 is notable for several attempts to come to terms with its recent past. For the film industry, a key development came regarding censorship, a practice that although less politically-motivated under Kim Young Sam, was still a major issue: even in 1995, only 59% of local features emerged from the ratings process without modifications of some sort (see the Korea Motion Picture Promotion Corporation's *Korean Cinema Yearbook* 1996).

On 4 October 1996, the Constitutional Court issued a ruling that government censorship of films and videos before their release was unconstitutional. The case had been brought to the court in 1993 by Kang Heon, producer of Jangsan-gotmae's aforementioned underground film *Oh! Land of Dreams*. The court's decision cleared the filmmakers of all criminal charges connected with its unauthorised 1988 screening, and forced a rewrite of the law to restrict the powers of the ratings board (see Bae 2005: 504). Struggles over censorship would not go away after the decision. In fact, in 1997 they ranked as one of the year's defining issues, given a ratings battle over Jang Sun-woo's antisocial *Bad Movie* (1997), an import block placed on Hong Kong director Wong Kar-Wai's *Happy Together* (*Chun gwong cha sit*, 1997), the banning of the inaugural Queer Film Festival and the arrest of Seoul Human Rights Film Festival director Seo Jun-shik under the National Security Law, for screening the Korean documentary *Red Hunt (Redeu heonteu*, 1996), about a 1948 civilian uprising on Jeju Island. Despite the continuing conflicts, however, the 1996 decision still stands as an important legal precedent and a symbolic milestone in the development of the Korean film industry.

Meanwhile, a much more dramatic court case took place earlier in the year, when the Kim Young Sam administration took the surprise decision to try former presidents Chun Doo Hwan and Roh Tae Woo in court. The two men were arrested and charged with mutiny and sedition for their roles in the 1979 military coup that established their power, and for the violence in Gwangju in 1980. Separately, they were also charged with creating gargantuan personal slush funds worth hundreds of millions of dollars during their years in office. An official investigation into Gwangju was launched prior to the trial, and television stations broadcast a host of documentaries revisiting the events of May 1980.

In August 1996, the Seoul District Court sentenced Chun to death and Roh to 22-and-a-half years in prison. An appeals court later reduced the sentences to life in jail and 17 years, respectively, and the two men would spend a year in jail before being pardoned in December 1997 at the urging of president-elect Kim Dae Jung.

These dramatic developments, and the media storm they unleashed, gave Koreans an opportunity to collectively start coming to terms with the darkest moments of the 1980s. However, on a smaller scale this process had already begun the previous year with the broadcast of the tremendously popular and influential television serial *Sandglass* (*Morae sigye*). Shown in 24 episodes over six weeks, the serial followed the lives of two men (a gangster played by Choi Min-soo and a prosecutor played by Park Sang-won) and one woman (a pro-democracy activist played by Ko Hyun-jeong) who become variously entangled in the politics and power hierarchies of the Chun Doo Hwan era. With its dramatic re-enactment of the Gwangju Uprising and broadly realistic depiction of the period's political and social oppressions, *Sandglass* brought Gwangju and other traumas of the 1980s into mainstream public debate for the first time since the end of military rule. The serial ranks as one of the most popular television shows ever screened in Korea, averaging a 45.3% viewer rating and peaking at 61.5% during its re-broadcast in early 1998 (see Lee 2005).

Meanwhile, another work from this period would re-examine the traumas of Gwangju, though in a far more controversial manner. Jang Sun-woo said that the desire to make a film about Gwangju was what originally drew him

The Gwangju uprising remembered in Jang
Sun-woo's *A Petal* (1996)

into the film industry. Ultimately, 15 years passed before he got the opportunity. In contrast to the television documentaries about the incident that were broadcast in 1996, *A Petal* presents a psychological and allegorical take on the tragedy. Jang describes the narrative as functioning in the same way as a *ssitkkim-gut*, a kind of shamanic ritual meant to relieve a burdened soul.

A Petal takes place some time after the massacre and focuses on a severely traumatised teenage girl, played by future pop star Lee Jung-hyun, who attaches herself to an abusive, disabled labourer Mr. Chang (Moon Sung-keun). Their relationship itself is a site of trauma: the man beats and rapes her, yet she – believing him to be her elder brother, at least initially – refuses to leave. As time goes on the man begins to feel shame and regret for his actions, and he too begins to show signs of psychological trauma. Violence pervades the film; like other of Jang's works, the characters exhibit strong sadistic or masochistic tendencies that complicate the viewer's identification with them. Viewers expecting a morally black-and-white depiction of innocent civilians and murderous government troops were taken aback, while feminist critics attacked Jang for his use of the rape-as-national-trauma metaphor, which by the mid-1990s had grown wearyingly familiar in Korean cinema. (Though it may be said in Jang's defence that his use of the metaphor is far more complex than that of his predecessors.) Jang says, 'I didn't want only to question the violence of the military regime which killed so many people in Gwangju in 1980. I thought we should also question the violence in ourselves ... It seems to me that there's a kind of inner violence, prevalent throughout society, and that we'll never solve our fundamental problems until we confront that' (quoted in Rayns 2007: 42–3).

The film's best-remembered scene is a flashback to the massacre, described at the start of this chapter. Here the trauma of the event is captured in heartbreaking fashion; it is one of the most intense and moving scenes in Korean cinema. Yet it is typical of Jang that this *ssitkim-gut* seems to provide little resolution. The girl vanishes at the film's end, and the labourer is left equally traumatised and unable to speak. In this film, the re-visiting and re-visualizing of trauma is more the working of human instinct than of a conscious effort to heal.

By 1996, Korean directors had secured at least a partial victory in their efforts to bring a new consciousness to local cinema, and to revisit the defining moments of the nation's recent past. Park Kwang-su's *A Single Spark (Areumdaun cheongnyeon jeontaeil,* 1995), about labour leader Jeon Tae-il's dramatic self-immolation in 1970, which helped to launch the modern labour movement, was another key milestone in this regard. It goes without saying that it would not have been possible for Park or Jang to shoot such films a decade earlier.

Korean cinema had changed in other ways too. In particular, the industrial environment in which films were created had transformed beyond recognition. From financing, distribution and marketing to production methods and government policy, Korean films were conceived, developed, produced and presented to audiences in an entirely new way. Inevitably, such changes had a profound effect on the style and content of films produced in the 1990s and beyond. The conditions that led to the film industry's restructuring, and the many implications of those changes, are considered in the next chapter.

2   A NEW FILM INDUSTRY

On 30 September and 1 October 1988, during the final days of the Seoul Olympics, live snakes were discovered on the floor of three movie theatres in Seoul screening Adrian Lyne's *Fatal Attraction*. Multiple screenings were cancelled, yet the film's distributor UIP declined to push for an investigation and the incident was not reported in the press. Several months later, on 16 February 1989, four young men carrying knives cut gashes in the screen at Sinyeong Theatre, which was presenting another UIP release, the James Bond film *The Living Daylights*. Then on 27 May, a cleaning woman discovered ten snakes and four containers of ammonia on the floor of the Cinehouse Theatre between screenings of UIP's third release, *Rain Man*. This time, police opened an investigation and the US Embassy lodged an official complaint with the South Korean government. Later in the summer, President George H. Bush responded to a letter from Korean film directors and warned against further acts of sabotage (see Lee Hyeong-gi 1989). However, on 13 August, a string of further incidents took place at six theatres in Seoul screening the UIP releases *Batteries Not Included* and *Indiana Jones and the Last Crusade*. At 4:30am, a Molotov cocktail thrown in an empty screening room at the Cinehouse Theatre destroyed ten seats and caused two million won ($2,300) worth of damage. Then at various times throughout the day, tear gas powder was dispersed at five theatres, sending viewers rushing for the exits (see Lee Yeon-ung 1989).

The Motion Pictures Association of Korea, which had been organising peaceful protests in front of Seoul movie theatres since September 1988, denied any connection with these incidents; however, it did release a statement saying, 'Until these theatres cancel their contracts with Hollywood branch offices, which are impeding the development of Korean cinema, such incidents will continue to occur' (quoted in Lee Yeon-ung 1989: 14). The following year, one director and one screenwriter were arrested in connection with the crimes; they were eventually released after serving seven months of a two-and-a-half year sentence.

Just as in the previous year activists had waged battles on the streets against the authoritarian power of the state, in 1988 filmmakers took up what they believed to be a life and death struggle over the fate of Korean cinema. Although the industry was facing multiple challenges at this time, from cooling audience interest to a crisis in film financing, most filmmakers believed the direst threat to be competition from Hollywood. And the nature of that competition had just shifted radically, with a change in film policy that permitted Hollywood branch offices to operate on Korean soil.

In the past, local films had been protected to some degree from competition against Hollywood through import quotas and other government regulations. The local market was closed to foreign distributors, who instead had to sell release rights to Korean companies. From 1988, however, US distributors such as UIP (which handled international distribution for Paramount, Universal and MGM/UA), Warner Bros., Twentieth Century Fox, Columbia and Disney received permission to establish branch offices in Seoul and to operate in the Korean market without restrictions. The Hollywood studios were well known for their aggressive distribution strategies, marketing know-how and seemingly unlimited financial resources. Many Korean film companies, by contrast, were on their last legs, as the system that had shaped their development since the early 1960s had started to crumble.

The old system

A close look at the policies that governed the Korean film industry from the 1960s to the mid-1980s paints a telling picture of how an authoritarian government exerts control. A year after taking power in the May 1961 coup, Park Chung Hee enacted the Motion Picture Law (*Yeonghwa-beop*), which served as the film industry's regulatory blueprint. The law covered various aspects of filmmaking, but one of its primary effects was to consolidate the film industry into a limited number of companies, and to make them dependent on the government for their long-term success. To make films, production companies were required to hold a licence from the government. Independent production was outlawed. Stringent requirements were also placed on the licensing process such that only the largest and best capitalised companies in the industry could comply. For example, the law (seemingly taking the old Hollywood studio system as its model) required film companies to own studio space, sound recording and laboratory facilities, a lighting system, at least three 35mm cameras and to have at least two full time directors and several full time actors under contract. Each company was also required to produce a minimum of 15 films per year (see Standish 1994: 73). As a result, only a few large companies were able to meet the requirements, and those that did took care to maintain a good relationship with the government.

If the licensing system was the stick, then the right to import foreign films was the carrot that kept film executives focused on the government's priorities. Only a small number of imports were allowed into the country each year; in the early 1980s, the annual average was about 20–25 films. Virtually all these films performed well at the box office, given that the restricted flow of Hollywood and foreign cinema created a pent-up demand. However the government provided companies with import permits for only one film at a time, and only after certain conditions were met. Although the specific terms changed almost on a yearly basis, some of the conditions companies had to meet in order to import one foreign film included: producing and releasing three Korean features; winning the top prize at the local Grand Bell Awards; winning an award at an international film festival; producing a film that earned the highest export dollars in a given year; or, in the 1970s especially, producing a 'quality film' (usu-yeonghwa) made to reflect government policies or priorities (see Bak Ji-yeon 2005: 241).

The basic philosophy behind the system was to force companies to reinvest their profits from imports back into local production. The measures were successful in ensuring that a large number of Korean films were produced in each year; however, it also gave producers no incentive to invest in infrastructure or to improve the quality of local films. If, as was the case with many film companies, the only reason to produce a Korean film was to move one step closer to securing an import permit, then it only made sense to produce it as quickly and cheaply as possible. The system failed to encourage the raising of technical standards (post-dubbing of dialogue tracks remained the norm all the way to the mid-1980s), and created a mindset that local films were fundamentally inferior to foreign cinema.

If there was one silver lining, it was that directors who were prepared to deal with rushed schedules and low production values that were endemic to the system – and to avoid trouble with censors – were free to shoot films with little interference from above or pressure to conform to commercial expectations. Some of the most interesting Korean films of the 1970s and 1980s, such as Kim Ki-young's *Iodo (Ieodo,* 1977, a work which ironically was classified as a 'quality film'), Kim Soo-yong's *Night Voyage (Yahaeng,* 1977) or Lee Jang-ho's *Declaration of Fools* display a creative energy and unpredictability that more than compensate for their low production values and lack of craftsmanship. Director Im Kwon-taek, for his part, found the freedom to distance himself from genre filmmaking and explore a new film aesthetic with the 'quality films' *The Genealogy (Jokbo,* 1978) and *The Hidden Hero* (*Gitbareomneun gisu,* 1979). Nonetheless, these were exceptional cases, and the majority of films produced in this period were little seen and soon forgotten. The local industry's failure to maintain even a minimal level of commercial quality was one of the factors behind a precipitous drop in annual theatrical admissions, from 166 million in 1970 to 44 million in 1984.

Policy revisions and the new producer

The Motion Picture Law was amended in 1963, 1966, 1970 and 1973, either to fix perceived faults in the system or (in 1973 especially) to strengthen government control even further, but the nature of the relationship between the government and the film industry remained constant. However, two more amendments adopted in the 1980s would, in contrasting ways, pave the way for the birth of a new film industry. The fifth revision, passed in December 1984 and put into effect in July 1985, freed up regulations concerning production and opened the door for a new generation of producers to enter the film industry. These reforms, which young producers had been requesting for years, did not represent a sudden change of heart on the part of the Chun administration; instead they served as a concession to the local industry in advance of the sixth revision, enacted in 1987, which opened the Korean film market to foreign competition. Both of these policy reforms would have a transformative effect in the long term, in ways that few observers could have predicted at the time.

The fifth revision of the Motion Picture Law contained three important reforms. The first was to replace the licensing system for production companies with a simple registration system, under which producers were required only to fill out certain forms and a provide a cash deposit (150 million won, reduced to 50 million in 1986). Companies were required to produce one feature film per year or else their registration would be annulled, but otherwise the government ceased to be involved in deciding which companies would be allowed to engage in production. Secondly, the revision legalised independent film production for companies or individuals who did not have the means or desire to officially register with the government. Up to one independent film per year could be produced, if a notice was submitted to authorities and certain capital requirements were met. Censorship procedures, of course, remained in place for independent films, but at one stroke this reform drastically lowered the barriers to entry for outsiders who wished to become involved in filmmaking. Finally, the third major change was to sever the link between film imports and local production, ending the days of the 'quota quickie'. In the coming years, virtually all official restrictions on film imports would be lifted.

The concrete effects of the fifth revision can be seen in the statistics: the number of domestic film production companies registered with the government jumped from 25 to 98 in the years 1985 to 1989. These figures do not include independents, so it is clear that a vast number of new producers entered the film industry in this period (see Jo 2005: 153).

Meanwhile, the number of imported films exploded. While only 25 foreign features were imported in 1984, by 1989 there were 264, more than a ten-fold increase. The higher numbers also resulted in a greater diversity in the origins, genres and styles of films. Among the 25 titles imported in 1984 were four from Hong Kong (including *Project A* and *Wheels on Meals*), one from Taiwan (*The Young Hero of Shaolin*), one Italian-US co-production (*Once Upon a Time in America*) and 19 from the US, including *E.T.: The Extra-Terrestrial* and *Terminator*. The totals from 1989 include 96 films from the US, 89 from Hong Kong, 26 from Italy, 13 from France, ten from Taiwan, six each from the UK and West Germany, two each from Argentina, China, Spain, Sweden and the USSR, and one each from Australia, Denmark, Indonesia, the Netherlands, Poland, Switzerland and Turkey.

	1984	1985	1986	1987	1988	1989	1990	1991	1992	1993	1994	1995
Korean films released	81	80	73	89	87	110	111	121	96	63	65	64
imported films released	25	27	50	84	175	264	276	256	319	347	382	359
total admissions (millions)	43.9	48.1	47.3	48.6	52.2	55.3	53.4	52.1	47.1	48.2	48.3	45.1
market share, domestic films (%)	38.5	34.2	33.0	27.0	23.3	20.2	20.2	21.2	18.5	15.9	20.5	20.9
screens	534	561	640	673	696	772	789	762	712	669	629	577
total exports (US $ '000s)	95.72	20	127.8	425.32	589.78	365.66	1579.33	472.85	195.90	173.84	620.88	208.68
avg. ticket price (won)	1532	1432	1533	1637	1847	2271	2602	3034	3471	3711	3895	4268
exchange rate (won/US$)	1065	1163	1169	1091	940	860	881	870	899	907	875	826

Table 1: Film industry statistics, 1984–95. Source: *Korean Cinema Yearbook*

However, one of the most far-reaching effects of the fifth revision was to open the door to a younger generation of producers, many of whom would bring new ideas and working methods that would be instrumental in modernising the industry. It may be instructive to compare and distinguish between the new producers and the new directors of this period. Both were, in a sense, trying to overcome the legacies of authoritarian rule: the New Wave directors were aiming to break free of old ideologies and launch a new, socially relevant cinema, while the producers had inherited a broken industry that had been misshaped by decades of harmful film policies. Producer Shin Chul asserts that in the late 1980s, 'Nobody was thinking about how to develop the film industry, the issue was merely to fight for survival' (interview with author, November 2008). But as time passed, producers and other industry figures would devote themselves with zeal to the building of a modern, smoothly functioning infrastructure that could support local cinema.

Shortly after the adoption of the fifth revision, another major reform shook the industry. Passed in December 1986 and enacted in July 1987, the sixth revision was the end result of a long process of negotiation with US trade representatives. The Motion Picture Export Association of America (MPEAA) had been lobbying for the opening of the Korean film market since the 1970s; however, it was only in the mid-1980s when – anxious to secure Korean automobile manufacturers greater access to the US market, and threatened with trade retaliation under the United States' infamous 'Super 301' clause – the Chun administration struck a deal.

The agreed-upon reforms were initially included in the first Korea-US Film Agreement of 1985, and later incorporated into the sixth revision. The biggest change, as noted above, was to grant foreign film companies the right to operate branch offices on Korean soil. This not only made it possible for the Hollywood studios to release their own films in Korea, it also gave them the opportunity to push for the modernisation of the Korean system from the inside. In addition to this concession, a government-imposed ceiling on prices paid for imported films was abolished, as well as a regulation that limited film companies to importing only one film per year. Various fees were also eliminated, including an import tax originally set at 150 million won per film, which was paid into the Domestic Film Promotion Fund. Finally, Korea agreed to gradually phase out a ten-print limit on the scale of theatrical releases, with a full liberalisation scheduled for 1994.

With the passage of these laws, what had formerly been one of the most regulated film markets in the non-Communist world was suddenly thrown open to foreign competition. Although local filmmakers had welcomed the deregulation of local production in the fifth revision, many were frightened that such a sudden market opening would overwhelm local industry. The film community first mobilised to campaign against the Korea-US Film Agreement, then lobbied for a delay so that the industry could find its feet before the full market opening. In the end, the government turned a blind eye to the petitions and rallies, and the reforms went ahead on schedule.

The one regulatory safeguard left in place at this time was a Screen Quota system that required all theatres in Korea to screen domestic films for a minimum number of days per year (106–146 days, depending on various factors). The aim of the quota was to ensure that local films received adequate screen time to reach their box-office potential. Although theatre owners opposed the system, since it obligated them to screen Korean films in place of higher-earning foreign titles, supporters argued that the quota was necessary to give local investors reassurance that the finished work would receive a reasonably-sized commercial release (see Yecies 2007). A decade later, the Screen Quota would re-emerge as a key point of contention between the Korean film industry and the MPEAA.

Changes wrought by the branch offices

The opening of branch offices by the Hollywood studios took place over a five-year period, beginning with UIP in March 1988, and followed by Twentieth Century Fox (August 1988), Warner Bros. (December 1989), Columbia Tristar (October 1990) and Buena Vista International/Disney (January 1993). Their presence in the Korean film market, together with the deregulation of film imports, would hasten the collapse of several aspects of the old system. In particular, the distribution sector – and by implication, the financing of Korean films – would never look the same again.

In previous decades, Korea's distribution/financing system had evolved in ways that that were not particularly efficient, but which allowed for business risk to be shared among multiple parties. The major filmmaking companies were based in the capital Seoul, and each operated one major theatre in the city centre that acted as a primary source of revenue. For example, Taehung Pictures, which produced films by Im Kwon-taek,

Jang Sun-woo and others, leased and operated Korea's oldest theatre Danseongsa. The company would release the Korean films it produced, as well as any foreign titles it was allowed to import, in this venue and retain the profits from ticket sales. However Taehung did not distribute nation-wide. South Korea was divided up into six other regional markets, based around the outer regions of Seoul, Gyeonggi/Gangwon, Chungcheong, Honam/Jeju, Gyeongbuk and Gyeongnam, which included Korea's second largest city Busan. In each of these markets, a number of regional dis-tributors (typically 5–7 per region) would book films into local theatres and arrange for marketing/publicity. For a typical release such as Lee Jang-ho's *Between the Knees*, Taehung would pre-sell the film to a regional distribu-tor in each market while the work was in pre-production. After gathering payment from the six regions, it would use this money to finance the film's production. Subsequently, upon its theatrical release, the local distribu-tors would keep the profits earned in each region (see Paquet 2005: 36).

The advantage of this system was that, from the Seoul-based pro-ducer's point of view, films could be made for less money up front, and the regional distributors would share in the risk that the work would fail com-mercially. Another issue was that companies in Seoul had little recourse to check the accuracy of admission figures supplied by the regional dis-tributors, whose murky and aggressive business dealings were the stuff of industry lore. While profit-sharing arrangements involved a real danger of being cheated, the pre-sell system (referred to derogatively by Korean com-mentators as *ipdo-seonmae* or the 'pre-harvest sale of rice') eliminated any need for transparency or trust.

However, after the passage of the fifth and sixth revisions, the old system quickly entered a period of upheaval. Firstly, the market became much more difficult to navigate for many of the regional distributors. In the past, virtually any of the foreign films allowed into the country could be expected to earn a decent return; however, after the deregulation of imports it became much more difficult to predict which films had a chance of success. At the same time, the number of local production and import companies expanded greatly, meaning that new business relationships and partnerships had to be established. By the late 1980s, many of the less savvy regional distributors were going out of business; for example the city of Gwangju saw its number of distributors shrink from six to three between 1987 and 1989 (see Jo 2005: 158–9).

The more fundamental challenge to the system was the gradual move towards nationwide distribution. The Hollywood branch offices had plenty of capital and were more interested in maximising their profits than in doling out risk. Nationwide distribution also potentially offered them more control over how their films would be marketed to audiences. As in other areas, UIP was the pioneer in this effort. Bypassing the regional distributors, UIP sought to establish direct and trustworthy business relationships with theatre owners across the country who would release their films. Although the process took longer than expected, by 1992 the company had assembled a nationwide distribution line made up of forty screens.

The other branch offices, for their part, tried out different sorts of partnerships and contracts with the older Seoul-based companies who were more experienced in distribution. One company in particular, Seoul Theatre, headed by Gwak Jeong-hwan, formed long-term partnerships with Warner Bros., Buena Vista and later Twentieth Century Fox, giving it an unmatched lineup of films that helped it to assemble its own strong nationwide distribution network. (In the mid-1990s, Seoul Theatre would form an alliance with Korean company Cinema Service, creating a powerful distributor that would eventually play a major role in local cinema's commercial renaissance.)

Such developments in distribution edged the Korean film sector closer to international business norms; however, it was also pushing Korean cinema into crisis. The flood of imports meant that domestic films were facing much steeper competition. At the same time, the regional distributors who had served as an important source of finance for Korean cinema over previous decades were moving towards irrelevancy. Whereas in 1984, domestic films sold 16.9 million tickets for a 38.5% share of the market, by 1993 (despite the success of *Sopyonje*) they had sunk to a modern-day low of 7.7 million tickets and a 15.9% market share. The branch offices, for their part, saw their share of the local market increase dramatically from year to year. A quote by critic Kim Hwa from the 1993 *Korean Cinema Yearbook* captures the despair felt by many local filmmakers in this era:

> The Korean film industry began the year 1992 without a single coin to inherit from the past, and in a state of self-examination, set off on a lonely battle for its existence. It was a year marked by grim determination and a lonely, desperate struggle for survival. (1993: 41)

Enter the 'chaebol'

Since the 1960s, South Korea's economy had been dominated by large, family-owned conglomerates known as *chaebol*. Sharing much in common with Japan's prewar *zaibatsu* (the two words also come from the same Chinese root), the *chaebol* prospered thanks to close ties to the government and easy access to state-guaranteed loans. Although active in a bewildering array of fields, by the 1980s the conglomerates were shifting their focus from chemicals, defence and heavy industries to electronics and high tech. It was the *chaebol*'s emergence as manufacturers of videocassette recorders that would eventually lead them to the film industry.

Korea put its first domestically-produced VCR on the market in 1979; however, by the mid-1980s it was clear that a lack of software (that is, pre-recorded videotapes) was holding back sales. Three of the *chaebol* – Samsung, Daewoo and SKC – responded by launching their own video divisions in 1984. Initially, the three companies sourced much of their content through exclusive video distribution deals with Hollywood studios, whereby the studios would sell the rights for a fixed price and the *chaebol* would produce the tapes and keep whatever profits were made (theatrical distribution was handled separately). However, this arrangement, lucrative for the *chaebol*, came unwound after the establishment of the branch offices. In 1988, UIP launched its own video distribution arm under the name CIC. Other branch offices were slower to follow UIP's lead, but by the early 1990s they had restructured their business partnerships with the *chaebol* so that the former would produce videos under their own label, and the *chaebol* would merely distribute to wholesalers for a small percentage of profits, typically 12–13% (see Hwang 2001: 81).

The *chaebol*, deprived of what had once been their greatest revenue source, instead had to compete with each other to secure rights to Korean productions, other foreign films or US titles that were not affiliated with a studio. Meanwhile, the video market as a whole entered a period of explosive growth from 1989–92. Total revenues from the rental market rose from 196 billion won in 1989 to 600 billion won (approximately $670 million) in 1992, while outright sales of videos (sell-through) rose from 40 billion won to 250 billion won ($280 million). Prices paid for video rights jumped accordingly, particularly for Korean films.

The 'planned film'
Marriage Story (1992),
partly financed by
Samsung

It was a matter of calculation that led Samsung to invest in its first Korean feature. Kim Ui-seok's *Marriage Story* (*Gyeorhon iyagi*, 1992), about a new generation couple whose marriage plunges into crisis as the wife's career takes off, was produced on a budget of 600 million won ($670,000). Samsung invested 150 million won, or 25%, in return for video rights, while producer Ikyoung Films retained theatrical, television and other rights. By investing before the film was made, Samsung was taking on the risk that the film would turn out to be a commercial flop; however, it obtained video rights for significantly less than the going rate for completed films. *Marriage Story* then turned out to be the top grossing Korean film of the year with a massive 520,000 admissions in Seoul. In the wake of this success story, Daewoo (which had considered but ultimately declined to invest in *Marriage Story*) and other conglomerates quickly followed suit, so that by mid-decade virtually all of the top-grossing Korean films had a *chaebol* investor.

Meanwhile, the *chaebol* found capable partners in the new generation of producers who had moved into the film industry following the fifth revision of the Motion Picture Law. It is unlikely that workable partnerships could have been formed with the old guard of producers who had dominated the industry during military rule, given concerns over the latter's trustworthiness and lack of fiscal transparency. Young, innovative and financially literate, the new producers were committed to making a new kind of film.

As time passed, the *chaebol* became more and more active in the film industry. After initially participating as partial investors, by 1995 they were providing 50% or 100% financing for many Korean films. Some examples of features that were 100% financed by the *chaebol* include Lee Min-yong's *A Hot Roof*, Kim Sang-jin's *Take the Money and Run* (*Doneul gatgo twieora*, 1995) and Lim Soon-rye's *Three Friends* (*Se chingu*, 1996) by Samsung; Park Kwang-su's *A Single Spark* and Lee Myung-Se's *Their Last Love Affair* by Daewoo; Kim Tae-kyun's *The Adventures of Mrs. Park* (*Bakbonggon gachulsageon*, 1996) by SKC; and Park Chul-soo's *Farewell My Darling* by Jinro (see Jo 2005: 186–8). As majority investors, the *chaebol* were now controlling all rights to their films, from the theatrical release to international sales. This was a significant change, because rather than simply providing finance and handling the video release, the *chaebol* were now intimately involved in all aspects of a film's commercial life span.

In this way, larger conglomerates started to expand into other sectors of the film business. Both Samsung and Daewoo built up nationwide distribution operations, which hastened even further the demise of the regional distributors. The two companies also leased, purchased or built theatres in Seoul and regional cities to operate themselves, and both were active in the cable television sector. The *chaebol* also formed strategic partnerships with young producers, which allowed the latter to launch and operate their own production companies. Examples include Uno Films (later renamed Sidus), Myung Films and Cinema Service with Samsung; Cine2000 with Daewoo; and Ahn's World Productions with SKC.

Thus by mid-decade, the biggest *chaebol* shared much in common with their primary competitors, the Hollywood branch offices. They were vertically integrated businesses that had a hand in nearly all aspects of a film's life cycle from investment and production to distribution, exhibition and ancillary markets like video and cable television. They used their considerable financial resources to give their product increased prominence in the marketplace, while at the same time attempting to shape and develop the film market as a whole. Their efforts to secure imported films for their lineup even led them to invest in the US. In early 1996 Samsung purchased a $60 million, 7.6% stake in New Regency, producer of Michael Mann's *Heat* (1995), giving it access to all the mini-major's films (see the Korea Motion Picture Promotion Corporation's *Korean Cinema Yearbook* 1996: 223), while in 1995 Cheil Jedang's new film division CJ Entertainment bought a $300 million, 11% founding stake in major studio DreamWorks (see Russell 2008).

The activities of the *chaebol* brought many changes to Korean cinema. One was a rise in film budgets, which was perhaps part intentional and part the natural result of an increased amount of capital in the industry. The average film cost roughly 500–600 million won to shoot in 1992, but by 1996 this had risen to 1.5–2 billion won. This was accompanied by a drop in the number of films produced in Korea each year, partly due to the difficulties faced by smaller, non-*chaebol* affiliated film companies. After producing about one hundred films a year from 1989 to 1992, the annual average fell to about sixty, where it would remain for the next decade.

The *chaebol*'s approach also magnified the importance of the local star system. Given their generally conservative approach to investing, many *chaebol* insisted on the casting of name stars in an effort to reduce risk. With top actors like Shim Eun-ha and Han Suk-kyu more in demand, salaries began to rise. From a creative standpoint, this also created a pre-disposition towards narratives that focused on one or two strong central characters rather than ensemble casts.

Although the *chaebol* would invest in many works by the better known auteurs of the Korean New Wave, they also showed a strong interest in genre cinema. The success of *Marriage Story* in 1992 inspired a string of further sex-war comedies, such as Kim Ui-seok's follow-up *That Woman, That Man* (*Geu yeoja, geu namja*, 1993) and Kang Woo-suk's *How to Top My Wife* (*Manura jugigi*, 1994). A large number of dramas about marriage and family, many starring the actress Choi Jin-sil, also appeared, including *Mom's Got a Lover* (*Eommaege aeini saenggyeosseoyo*, 1995), *Ghost Mama* (*Goseuteu mama*, 1996) and *Baby Sale* (*Beibi seil*, 1997). Nonetheless, the *chaebol*'s film divisions were often criticised for taking an overly formulaic approach that failed to significantly diversify commercial Korean cinema.

Shin Chul and the 'planned film'

One of the ways in which Korea's young producers attempted to survive in the now highly competitive local market was to introduce new methods of developing and producing films. One of the most influential figures in this regard was Shin Chul, a member of the 'cultural centre generation' who, while overseeing marketing at the Piccadilly Theatre in Seoul in the mid-1980s, was able to meet and interview large numbers of ordinary viewers. This experience, which he called 'eye-opening', led him to push for a new model of commercial filmmaking that would incorporate a far more detailed knowledge of viewers' perspectives and tastes into the screenwriting process. Observers would eventually refer to this type of work as the 'planned film' (*gihoek yeonghwa*).

The planned film involved the early identification of a target audience, the use of market research and a long period of script development and pre-production (none of which was widely practised at the time) to improve a film's chances of success. An increased focus was also placed on marketing from the early stages of a project. The first feature to be labelled as a planned film was Kang Woo-suk's *Happiness Does Not Depend on School Records* (*Haengbogeun seongjeok suni anijanayo*, 1989), starring Lee Mi-yeon as a high school girl at the top of her class who commits suicide due to pressure over grades. Shin's company Shincine, launched in 1988 as a dedicated planning company, partnered with production house HwangKiSung Films on the project. Shin then interviewed over 500 high school students over a year-and-a-half and worked with screenwriter Kim Seong-hong to incorporate many of their ideas and experiences into the script. Shin describes how midway through development producer Hwang Ki-sung nearly pulled out of the project:

> Hwang had originally liked the concept, but as time passed and no screenplay appeared (because we continued to rewrite it), he began to lose faith in it. The regional distributors were also telling him there was no demand for this type of film. I tried to persuade him to keep the project running, but he refused, so finally I picked ten of the high school kids we had interviewed and I asked Hwang simply to buy them dinner, and then I'd stop bothering him. He took them to a nearby pork restaurant and had a two-hour talk with them, and after it was done he came to me and said, 'I think we need to make this movie.' (Interview with author, November 2008)

The film was a commercial success, with over 155,000 Seoul admissions, and soon other companies began to give greater weight to planning. As Shin notes, the production system in use at that time placed the majority of responsibility on three figures: the director, the line producer who would oversee the shoot and the executive producer who would secure financing. In most cases, the director would have to assume responsibility for both the aesthetic quality and the commercial marketability of the final product. Under the new system, the individual who was given a 'planning' (*gihoek*) credit took on increased responsibility for developing the film's commercial potential. 'We were not working off any foreign models at the time, but eventually I realised that in standard filmmaking practice, this was basically the role of the producer,' says Shin (interview with author, November 2008).

It was with Shincine's next project, the aforementioned *Marriage Story,* that the planned film enjoyed its highest profile success. Targeting female viewers, Shin interviewed countless numbers of young married couples and employed eight screenwriters to perform 16 rewrites of the script. After the huge success of the project, Shincine began producing films on its own, rather than complement the work of other production companies. Its first in-house production, the Daewoo-financed *Mister Mama (Miseuteo mama,* 1992), about a husband left to raise his baby daughter after his wife runs off, was a solid hit with 230,000 Seoul admissions. The success of that work helped to establish two more companies: producer/director Kang Woo-suk launched Cinema Service, which would later evolve into a major studio, and co-producer Yu In-taek launched Keyweck-shidae (literally, 'Age of Planning'), which would produce *A Single Spark, Resurrection of the Little Match Girl* and *May 18 (Hwaryeohan hyuga,* 2007). In general, Shincine's early films are famous for gathering together figures who would eventually become the industry's most powerful producers. Tcha Seung-jae, future head of Sidus FNH, served as production manager on *Mister Mama*; Shim Jae-myung (aka Jaime Shim), who would co-launch Myung Films and produce *JSA, The Isle (Seom,* 2000) and *A Good Lawyer's Wife (Baramnan gajok,* 2003), oversaw marketing on *Marriage Story*; and Oh Jung-wan, who would launch b.o.m. Film Productions and produce *Untold Scandal (Seukaendeul,* 2003), *A Bittersweet Life (Dalkomhan insaeng,* 2005) and *Night and Day (Bamgwa nat,* 2007), was producer on *Marriage Story.*

Ultimately, the introduction of planned films can be seen as representing not just a reform of standard production methods, but also an effort to reconnect with mainstream viewers. Many of the films of the 1970s and 1980s were made with different audiences in mind. The 'quality films' of the 1970s, and many of the 'quota quickies' of the 1980s, were essentially made for government bureaucrats. Some critics charged that many of the period-set dramas of the 1980s were designed to appeal to international film festival programmers. The films of the Korean New Wave were ostensibly made for the *minjung*, but their formal experimentation and political orientation served to alienate many ordinary viewers. In this sense, not only the method but also the mindset behind planned films – perhaps best encapsulated by Shin's anecdote about Hwang's dinner with the students – was something new.

On the whole, local cinema continued to be held in low regard by most of the populace throughout the mid-1990s. In an effort to attract viewers, producers and directors experimented, attempting difficult-to-produce genres (period sci-fi epic *The Gate of Destiny* (*Gwicheondo*, 1996)), overseas locations (*Inch'Allah* (*Insyalla*, 1996), set in Algeria and shot in Morocco) or special effects (Shincine's *The Fox With Nine Tails* (*Gumiho*, 1994), Korea's first film to feature computer-generated imagery). Although many of these failed to turn a profit, they helped young producers gain experience and establish a foothold within the industry. On a technical level, young crew members improved their skills and learned from their mistakes. The Korean film industry had not enjoyed especially strong success in the early- to mid-1990s, but it had set the stage for a startling commercial revival that would arrive sooner than anyone expected.

3   THE BOOM

The boom began with a crash. Confidence in the Korean economy had withered in the autumn of 1997, with the nation's *chaebol* struggling under gargantuan levels of debt, banks weighed down by non-performing loans, and many individual companies (including, most prominently, carmakers Kia and Samsung Motors) facing bankruptcy. A full-blown financial crisis in Thailand over the summer had stoked fears that the contagion might spread across Asia and, sure enough, in November the Korean financial system experienced meltdown. The stock market plunged as it became clear that Korean banks were unable to pay back billions of dollars worth of short-term foreign debt, and that the government lacked the resources to rescue them. After several weeks of trying to hide the full extent of the problem, the Kim Young Sam administration announced on 22 November that, in order to avoid a default, it would ask the International Monetary Fund (IMF) for a massive bailout.

The following months were a time of chaos. Ratings agency Moody's downgraded Korea's sovereign debt rating to junk status on 22 December. That same week, the Korean currency sank to an all-time low of 1640 won to the dollar, from 965 at the start of November. On 1 January, the government asked its citizens to donate gold and jewellry to help it repay its debts; according to organisers, ten tons of gold were collected in the first two days (Anon. 1998). Meanwhile the IMF, which had assembled the record $57 billion rescue package, attached strict conditions to the loans. Interest rates were pushed as high as 30%, causing many companies to go bankrupt, and the IMF dictated broad restructuring of the corporate and banking sectors, as well as changes to labour laws. Unemployment rose from 2.8% to 8.2% in less than a year. Some international economists would later criticise the IMF for prescribing overly harsh medicine that may have only made the situation worse.

As the crisis raged, Korea held its third presidential election of the democratic era on 18 December. After losing the previous two contests, opposition leader Kim Dae Jung prevailed, pulling out a narrow 39.7% victory in a three-way contest. Kim's inauguration in February 1998 marked the first peaceful transfer of power between ruling and opposition parties in modern Korean history.

Thus began the 'IMF era', a time of wrenching economic pain and humiliation that put millions out of work and noticeably thinned the ranks of Korea's middle class. An estimated 20,000 companies went bankrupt in 1998, and the nation's economy shrank by 5.8% (see Robinson 2007: 173). Among the thirty largest *chaebol*, eleven would eventually collapse, including Daewoo in 1999 with $80 million in unpaid debt. A deep pessimism for Korea's future prospects settled over the populace.

The financial crisis also proved to be the death knell for many of the *chaebol*'s film divisions. Feeling political and economic pressure to shed unneeded subsidiaries and focus on core businesses, SKC closed its video and film divisions in January 1998, followed by Daewoo in January 1999 and Samsung in May 1999. The IMF crisis had seemingly robbed the film industry of its biggest investors at one stroke. However, as Hwang Dong-mi notes, even before the crisis hit, rumours were circulating that many *chaebol* were planning an exit (2001: 29–30). Profits, both for traditional theatrical/video releases and for new windows like cable television, had failed to meet original expectations. Imports, which in the early years had provided the film divisions with their most stable source of revenue, had become less profitable after fierce competition between Korean buyers pushed up prices by 50%. The box-office failure of several big-budget productions like CJ Entertainment's *Inch'Allah*, Daewoo's *Firebird* (*Bulse*, 1997) and SKC's *Ivan the Mercenary* (*Yongbyeongiban*, 1997) had caused many *chaebol* to switch from majority to minority investing in local films. Indeed, LG had already pulled out of the film industry in late 1996.

With the *chaebol* on their way out, only 43 local features were released in 1998, the lowest level since 1957. However, in contrast to the early 1990s, the mood in the film industry was cautiously buoyant. Optimists could point to several factors. For one, despite a slide in production, admissions to Korean films continued to rise. Boosted by hits such as Chang Youn-hyun's Internet romance *The Contact* (*Jeopsok*, 1997) and Lee Jeong-guk's melodrama *The Letter* (*Pyeonji*, 1997), which was enjoying a strong run in theatres even as the financial crisis was playing out, 59 local releases sold 12.1 million tickets in 1997 for a 25.5% market share. The following year, a mere 43 features sold 12.6 million tickets for a 25.1% share. Furthermore, a majority of the hit films in these years had secured financing not from the *chaebol* but from other sources, such as Kang Woo-suk's Cinema Service or Ilshin Investment, the first venture capital company to invest in Korean film.

Secondly, when the Korean currency crashed, the comparative costs and merits of domestic and imported films suddenly shifted. For example, SKC had purchased Korean rights to the Hollywood film *Seven Days in Tibet* in early 1997 for $3.5 million. When the contract was signed, this was equivalent to 2.8 billion won, but at the time payment was due it took 5 billion won to purchase the same amount of dollars. Not surprisingly, many large and small Korean companies wasted no time in closing their film acquisition departments. Local films, in contrast, began to seem like a more stable investment. Although the cost of making them had not lowered, the average 1998 budget of 1.2 billion won ($900,000) before print and advertising fees began to look more reasonable compared to the cost of acquiring a foreign film, and investors had no need to worry about currency fluctuations. In addition, any export revenues the films earned would be worth more in local currency. Exports of Korean films were still rare in the late 1990s, but the figures were rising: *The Gingko Bed* (*Eunhaengnamu chimdae*, 1996), for example, earned $500,000 from sales to Hong Kong, China, Singapore and other Asian countries (see Nam 1997).

The age of debut directors: 1996–2000

The biggest grounds for optimism, however, lay in the content. By 1998 it was becoming clear that a younger generation of directors was bringing a distinctly new aesthetic to Korean cinema. Youth-oriented, genre-savvy, visually sophisticated and not ashamed of its commercial origins, the New Korean Cinema of the late 1990s was perceived by Korean audiences as being something entirely different from the works that preceded it.

Kim Jee-woon's debut film, the horror-comedy *The Quiet Family* (1998)

The Quiet Family (*Joyonghan gajok*, 1998), the debut feature by director Kim Jee-woon, is a representative example of how the new films contrasted with the old. Set in a family-run lodge located alongside a hiking trail, the film focuses on the increasingly desperate actions of the owners when their lodgers keep turning up dead. Shifting back and forth between comedy, suspense and a dull sense of dread as the bodies pile up, the film exhibits a playful, carefree attitude at the same time as it shows how one act of violence can quickly lead to more. Meanwhile, a misprint on a signboard early in the film identifies the lodge as a 'safe house', a 1970s term referring to homes used by intelligence agents for interrogations and other secret operations. Film critic Kim Hyung-seok argues that, given this and other references, the eerie space of the lodge is meant to evoke the horrors of 1970s Korean politics (2008: 27–9).

On a visual level, *The Quiet Family* looked markedly different from its cinematic predecessors. Shot in rich, saturated colours, the film prioritised the use of lighting and set design to create memorable visual compositions rather than to capture the locale in any realistic manner. The opening shot, an exhilarating Steadicam sequence that meanders from the second floor down the stairs and onto the first before turning and retracing its steps, introduces the layout of the lodge but also clearly revels in its own technical bravado. If the visuals of the Korean New Wave functioned to ground the work in reality, the new directors were more likely to view visual expression in abstract terms, or as an end in itself.

Most notable about the film in the context of its time was its eclectic approach to genre. *The Quiet Family*'s casual appropriation and juxtaposition of genre conventions – from the lighting effects of horror to the broad physical movements of slapstick comedy – set it apart from both the commercial and art-house traditions of Korean filmmaking. Kim was not the only one practising such genre alchemy: in its wrap-up of the year 1998, film magazine *Cine21* named 'genre diffusion' as the first of ten key issues that had defined the year (Anon. 1999). On one level, New Korean Cinema grew out of a sincere love for genre films of all sorts. And yet for directors such as Kim, genre remained an object to be manipulated rather than a model to be followed. The enigmatic and open-ended conclusion of *The Quiet Family* violates the conventions of both the horror and comedy genres. Kim was borrowing from genre cinema, but also felt comfortable in adopting a narrative structure that was closer to art-house cinema than to mainstream commercial filmmaking.

In short, the new directors were cinephiles. Having been active participants in the cinephile movement of the early- to mid-1990s, which encompassed a broad range of cinema from European auteurs to Hong Kong action films, Taiwanese art cinema and Hollywood B-movies, they were now ready to incorporate these influences into local films. Audiences, for their part, proved highly receptive to such an approach. The sudden spread of foreign cinema in domestic film culture a decade earlier had found its way back into Korean cinema.

Korean film critic Kim Young-jin has referred to the energy that animated this movement as 'the adventurous spirit of children without fathers' (2007b: ix). Compared to countries like France or Japan where a rich and well-preserved film heritage maintains a strong hold on the national imagination, in Korea local classics exerted only a weak influence at best. Younger generation filmmakers 'are unable to claim affiliation to any lineage within film history, but at the same time they show a sponge-like resilience where they can assume whichever lineage suits them', says Kim (ibid.).

This is not to say that older Korean films had no influence on the new generation. Major filmmakers including Bong Joon-ho and Park Chan-wook (who in this period was better known as a film critic writing in support of underappreciated B-movies and art-house works) have acknowledged a strong debt to the maverick Korean director Kim Ki-young, who under the military regime produced such brilliant classics as *The Housemaid* (*Hanyeo*, 1960), *Insect Woman* (*Chungnyeo*, 1972) and *Iodo* (1978). 1970s Korean genre films, including spy flicks and so-called 'Manchurian Westerns', would also influence directors such as Ryoo Seung-wan and Kim Jee-woon. However, the key point is that these directors approached these works as cinephiles in search of inspiration, and not as filmmakers struggling to find a place for themselves within a dominant national tradition.

Another quality that set the new directors apart from the previous generation was a sense of distance from the traumas of the 1980s. E J-yong (Yi Jae-yong), director of *An Affair* (*Jeongsa*, 1998), *Asako in Ruby Shoes* (*Sunaebo*, 2000) and *Untold Scandal*, touched on the difference between the two movements when he said, 'Filmmakers from the 80s and 90s, like Park Kwang-su, Jang Sun-woo and Chung Ji-young, carry a great burden on their shoulders, in terms of history and politics. So they make very "heavy" films, and they can't free themselves from the weight of their generation's social issues. But directors in my generation feel free of such pressures. They pursue individual interests, rather than make films that speak for Korean society' (in Paquet 2003). This is not to imply that the new directors did not take on socially relevant themes or revisit the events of recent history. Indeed, this was a vein that was mined often, and Kim Young-jin asserts that 'though they might make films in a manner that appears playful, they also aim at a spirit of rebellion capable of provoking the group consciousness of the times' (2007b: ix). Usually, however, the social concerns of new generation directors were concealed within a genre framework or else, like *The Quiet Family*, were presented to audiences in a veiled fashion.

The young directors of this era had chosen an auspicious time to make their debut. Given the troubled history of local films, and their long-standing weakness at the box office, producers gave young directors a clear mandate to break from the past and forge a new identity for Korean cinema. Particularly interested in targeting the large youth market (viewers in their mid-30s or above made up a comparatively small percentage of moviegoers), producers encouraged new themes and a diversification of subject matter, and proved generally willing to tolerate experimentation in form and genre. Given this atmosphere of creative licence, it is probably no coincidence that almost all of the biggest names in New Korean Cinema debuted within this five year period: Hong Sang-soo, Kim Ki-duk and Kang Je-gyu in 1996; Lee Chang-dong in 1997; Kim Jee-woon and Im Sang-soo in 1998; and Bong Joon-ho in 2000. In contrast, no Korean director who debuted between 1990 and 1995 would go on to build a major international career, with the exception of Park Chan-wook, who did not establish himself until his third feature *Joint Security Area* in 2000.

Changes in film education

Another development that led to a diversification of styles and approaches in New Korean Cinema was the spread of film schools in the 1990s. Previously, most directors received their training under an apprentice system that involved working as an assistant to a more established filmmaker before making one's debut. Although several university-level film production departments existed in the 1970s and early 1980s (in 1980 there were four: Dongguk University, Chung-Ang University, Hanyang University and the Seoul Institute of the Arts), director Park Kwang-su explains that the curricula at such schools were focused on abstract and experimental film, and therefore graduates rarely, if ever, entered the mainstream film industry (interview with author, August 2008).

In 1984, the creation of the state-supported Korean Academy of Film Arts (KAFA), which offered a two-year programme in practical filmmaking skills, opened up a new path to joining the industry. The first graduating class included many future directors including Park Chong-won (*Kuro Arirang*) and Kim Ui-seok (*Marriage Story*). In the 1990s especially KAFA would emerge as the industry's leading source of talent, with a list of alumni that includes Bong Joon-ho (*Memories of Murder*), Im Sang-soo (*The President's Last Bang*), Hur Jin-ho (*Christmas in August*) (*Palworui keuriseumaseu*, 1998), Jang Joon-hwan (*Save the Green Planet*) (*Jigureul jikyeora*, 2003) and Choi Dong-hoon (*Tazza: The High Rollers*) (*Tajja*, 2006). The example set by KAFA also encouraged the opening of new university film programmes and the adoption of more practical-based approaches at existing departments. The number of film production departments at Korean universities stood at nine in 1989, 17 in 1996, 29 in 1999 and 52 in 2007 (see the Korean Film Council's *Korean Cinema Yearbook*). One particularly influential programme would be in the film department at the Korean National University of Arts, which opened in 1995 and which would turn out directors such as Jeong Jae-eun (*Take Care of My Cat*) (*Goyangireul butakae*, 2001) and Na Hong-jin (*The Chaser*) (*Chugyeokja*, 2008). At the same time, an increasing number of young Korean directors went abroad to receive their training, including Hong Sang-soo at the Art Institute of Chicago, Song Il-gon and Moon Seung-wook at the Polish National Film School in Lodz and Min Boung-hun at the Russian State Institute of Cinematography (VGIK).

The shift from an apprentice-based system of film training to more formal education in film schools helped to create a higher level of technical expertise among debut directors and cinematographers. It also gave film school graduates the opportunity to showcase their talent through short films. Producers, as well as directors looking for capable assistants, began to attend short film festivals and public screenings of graduation films from KAFA or the Korean National University of Arts in order to scout talent. It was the steady production of new filmmaking talent that allowed Korea to turn out an eye-opening number of debut directors each year. Many producers displayed a preference for working with first-time directors, partly because of their lower salaries and partly because they were perceived as being more likely to compromise over the final cut, in an industry that traditionally granted the director strong creative control. The year 2002 was typical: of 59 major theatrical releases, 31 or 53% were by debut directors.

The new system also proved to be more open to women. Excluding documentaries, only three women made their debut in the commercial film industry in the 1990s: Lim Soon-rye with the critically acclaimed *Three Friends* in 1996, *301/302* scriptwriter Lee Seo-gun with *Rub Love* (*Reobeureobeu*) in 1997 and KAFA graduate Lee Jeong-hyang with the popular hit *Art Museum by the Zoo* (*Misulgwanyeop dongmurwon*) in 1998. However, from 2001 to 2007 no less than 22 female directors saw their feature debut receive a commercial release. The new system promoted diversity in other ways as well. Director E J-yong, whose KAFA graduation short *Homo Videocus* (co-directed with Daniel H. Byun) won awards at the Clermont-Ferrand and San Francisco film festivals in 1990, argues that he too would have been unlikely to make his debut under the old system, given producers' propensity to favour extroverted, 'macho' personality types (in Paquet 2003).

The battle over the Screen Quota

Meanwhile controversy was brewing over Korea's Screen Quota system. Although on the books in various forms since 1966 (for a detailed examination see Yecies 2007), the quota emerged as the film industry's central pro-

A Screen Quota
protest in mid-1999
(Photo courtesy of
Cine21)

tective measure against imported films in the mid-1980s, when other import
barriers were removed. The system was designed to ensure that Korean
films as a whole received a minimum amount of screening time in local
theatres. Exhibitors were required to show domestic films on each screen
for at least 30–40% of the year, or else face suspensions. Specifically, the
base quota was set at 146 days per year (40%), but the Ministry of Culture
and Tourism was at liberty to provide a reduction of twenty days each year
(which it consistently granted), and each theatre could lower its individual
quota by a further twenty days by screening local films during peak seasons, such as the summer and winter school vacations.

As the audience for local films continued to shrink in the early 1990s,
observers suspected that, with the culture ministry showing little inclination to enforce the measure, most theatres were not fulfilling their quota
obligations. Taking matters into their own hands, in January 1993 film
industry activists formed a group called the Screen Quota Watchers, which
sent members out to major theatres each day to check in person which
films were being screened. At the end of the year, the group announced
that the average theatre had over-reported the extent to which it had
screened Korean films by 48 days. In the coming years, the Screen Quota
Watchers would use such statistics to publicise the issue and to pressure
the government to enforce the measure. In 1994, the gap between the average theatre's reported number of screening days for Korean films and the
actual number was 51.7 days, followed by 37.6 days in 1996, 20.5 days

in 1997, and 10.8 days in 1998 (Anon. 2001: 8; no figures published for 1995). This steady decline can be attributed to the Quota Watchers' efforts, although the rising popularity of Korean cinema surely played a major role as well.

However, throughout this period Hollywood lobbyists, led by the MPA's (formerly MPEAA) Jack Valenti, were pushing forcefully for the abolition of the Screen Quota. Arguing that the system was a violation of free trade principles, in 1998 US trade officials placed the quota on a list of items to be discussed in negotiations for a South Korea-US bilateral investment treaty. In July of that year, Korea's trade minister indicated that the government was leaning towards abolishing the quota. Members of the film industry reacted at once, forming an emergency committee, holding press conferences and staging protests in front of theatres.

Then in November, Korean trade negotiators proposed a reduction of the quota to 92 days – which their US counterparts rejected, hoping for a full repeal. In response, filmmakers took to the streets for the first time in a decade. Close to one thousand actors, directors, crew members and students participated in a march through central Seoul on 1 December, while on the same day, a group of top producers began a series of sit-ins at Myeongdong Cathedral (epicentre of the 1987 pro-democracy movement) which would ultimately last more than two months. The protests received wide coverage in the local press, not the least due to the star power involved, and polls showed that the public sympathised with the filmmakers. A group of twenty citizens' groups and NGOs also made public statements on behalf of the Screen Quota.

President Kim Dae Jung later announced his intention to keep the quota at its current level, which partially diffused the sense of crisis. However, in the coming months (and years), protests would continue at intervals as further announcements by various government figures seemed to hint at an imminent decision. The following June, in an even more photogenic display, 117 producers and directors including Im Kwon-taek and Kang Je-gyu shaved their heads in a rally held across the street from the US Embassy. Supporters of the quota, in keeping with similar cultural diversity movements across the globe, insisted that film as a cultural product should be excluded from trade negotiations. Demonstrators also argued (likely expecting it would never happen) that the quota should be kept at its current level until Korean cinema captured a 40% share of the local market.

The birth of the Korean blockbuster: Shiri and JSA

The projected image of Korean cinema in the Screen Quota protests was of a fragile, vulnerable industry. One of the most memorable photos from the December 1998 rally, reproduced on the cover of *Cine21*, was of actress Shim Eun-ha and other top stars dressed in black, carrying their own funeral portraits (an image that also recalled the critically acclaimed *Christmas in August*, released earlier that year). However, in February 1999 Korean cinema would present a very different image of itself to the world with the release of Kang Je-gyu's action blockbuster *Shiri* (*Swiri*, 1998).

Depicting a face-off between South Korean intelligence agents and a renegade group of North Korean special forces who are plotting a terrorist attack in Seoul, *Shiri* quickly established itself as a must-see film: Korea's first *bona fide* event movie since *Sopyonje*. It offered big-budget spectacle, special effects, star power (primarily in the casting of the lead from *The Contact*, Han Suk-kyu, though it also featured future stars Song Kang-ho, Choi Min-sik and Kim Yun-jin), and a politically resonant theme. Its box-office performance was unprecedented – the film vaulted over *Sopyonje*'s domestic record in 22 days and ended its four-month run with 6.21 million tickets sold nationwide (equivalent to $27.6 million). It had been made for 2.7 billion won ($2.3 million), which although high by the standards of the day would leave investors awash in profits.

Distributed by Samsung Entertainment as one of its final releases, *Shiri* featured shootouts on urban streets, exploding buildings, car chases, ticking bombs and other narrative/visual clichés of big-budget action films from Hollywood or Hong Kong. At the same time it incorporated a melodramatic love story between a South Korean agent and a North Korean spy that played off of Korea's collective anxiety over its long-standing political division. The film borrowed liberally from the model of the Hollywood blockbuster, but in addressing Korean themes it sought to be recognised and accepted as a local work.

Here, perhaps, was the sort of product envisioned by Kim Young Sam after hearing the *Jurassic Park*/Hyundai cars presentation in 1994. Not only did it break records in Korea, but it secured a highest-ever sale to Japan for $1.3 million, and it performed well in commercial releases throughout Asia. *Shiri* had achieved blockbuster status not only through its style and content but in the way in which (helped by a wide release and an aggressive marketing campaign) it was experienced as a shared cultural/media event. Indeed, in future years the phenomenon surrounding *Shiri*'s release would remain far more discussed than the film itself.

Many also viewed the work as a political text. Although the North Korean special forces were depicted as ruthless killing machines, the film allowed viewers a glimpse into their perspective, most famously in a monologue delivered by Choi Min-sik ('How can you, who grew up eating Coke and hamburgers, understand that your brothers in the North are starving?'), and in the sympathetic character of the undercover North Korean agent who infiltrates the South's operations. To that date, Korean filmmakers had still not yet taken advantage of relaxed censorship to present rounded characters from modern-day North Korea. At a time when president Kim Dae Jung was moving forward with his 'Sunshine Policy' built on engagement with the North, the film came across as both timely and relevant. (Jang Jin's *The Spy* (*Gancheop richeoljin*, 1999), released a month later, was also notable in this respect.)

In its cinematic style, marketing and its ultimate success *Shiri* left an unmistakable mark on Korean film history. Director Kang Je-gyu, who had already scored a box-office hit with *The Gingko Bed* in 1996, became recognised as one of the industry's commercial titans (and he took this opportunity to launch his own production/distribution/exhibition company KangJeGyu Films). However, *Shiri*'s most lasting effect may have been to impart to the industry a sense of expanding possibilities and self-confidence. Projects that may have seemed overly risky or ambitious a year earlier began to be perceived as lying within reach.

Meanwhile, a second Korean blockbuster would emerge in September 2000. Directed by the little known critic/filmmaker Park Chan-wook, *Joint Security Area* (or *JSA*) structured its narrative around a shooting incident at the border between North and South Korea. After a Swiss investigator named Sophie Jean (Lee Young-ae) arrives to mediate between North and South and their conflicting reports of the incident, the film moves into an extended flashback which reveals that two Northern and two Southern soldiers had met in secret and formed a close friendship in the weeks leading up to the deadly shootings. With both sides throwing obstacles in her path, Jean soon realises that she is charged with uncovering a truth that neither side wants to acknowledge.

The blockbuster *Joint Security Area* (2000) launched the career of Park Chan-wook

Like *Shiri*, *JSA* featured a well-known cast (Song Kang-ho, Lee Byung-hun, Lee Young-ae), a large budget (3 billion won before print and advertising costs, close to one third of which was spent on a 90% replica of the border village Panmunjeom), and a politically timely theme centred on North-South relations. It also duplicated *Shiri*'s success at the box office, with 5.83 million tickets sold after four months on release. (In 1999, *Shiri*'s total admissions were calculated as 5.8 million, but in April 2001 KangJegyu Films revised its estimate of *Shiri*'s total to 6.2 million.) A flood of news stories covered every aspect of the film's production and box-office performance, and the following February it was invited to screen in competition at the Berlin International Film Festival, where journalists drew comparisons to Germany and Berlin's own history as divided entities.

If *Shiri* more obviously utilised Hollywood conventions to stage and explore Korea-specific themes, *JSA* (which was based on a bestselling novel) displays a wider range of influences in presenting its complex story. The narrative itself is structured as a mystery; however, Park himself refers to this as a 'MacGuffin' meant to temporarily distract viewers from the heart of the story (quoted in? Kim Young-jin 2007b: 80). By the time the mystery's secret is revealed, it carries little emotional force because the characters have come to dominate the story.

Politically, *JSA* goes far beyond *Shiri* in humanising characters from the North. The nuanced acting of Song Kang-ho as Sergeant Oh and Shin Ha-kyun as Private Jung cause the viewer to forcefully identify with their characters, perhaps to an even greater extent than with the Southern soldiers. In doing so, the film creates a tension between the realm of the personal, in which the soldiers forge a close friendship, and the political, in which both sides remain sworn enemies. It is the seeming irreconcilability between these two realms that gives the film's dramatic conclusion its potency. At the same time it inevitably leads viewers to question the existing political framework.

The makers of *JSA* benefited from fortuitous timing, in that just three months prior to the film's release a historic summit took place in Pyongyang between South Korean president Kim Dae Jung and North Korean leader Kim Jong Il. The meeting represented the most dramatic warming in North-South relations in the two countries' history, and raised hopes that more than four decades of open aggression might finally be nearing an end. Later developments would dash such hopes, but *JSA* arrived in theatres just as many South Koreans were rethinking their attitudes towards the North, and the film functioned as a site of reflection upon such issues.

Julian Stringer describes the word 'blockbuster' as 'a moving target – its meaning is never fixed or clear, but changes according to who is speaking and what is being said' (2003: 2). Although some general notions surrounding the blockbuster are enduring, such as their size in relation to other films, their positioning as 'event movies' and their use of spectacle, Stringer argues that they are best understood as a genre. In this sense they are subject to the same kinds of internal and external struggles as other genres over their defining characteristics and boundaries.

In Korea as well, the meaning of the term blockbuster (transliterated from English into Korean and adopted as a loan word) has evolved over time, especially when referring to local productions. The first domestic film to lay claim to the term 'Korean-style blockbuster' in its marketing was Park Kwang-choon's *The Soul Guardians* (*Toemarok*) in 1998. Financed by Samsung, the film was based on a popular Internet novel about a young woman who had the ability to resurrect an evil supernatural force. Although notable for its advances in the field of computer-generated imagery (and many of the artists who rendered its CGI shots went on to found leading special effects companies in the coming years), the poorly-reviewed film fell short of expectations at the box office, and its marketers' efforts to define the work as a new type of film failed.

It was with *Shiri* and *JSA*, both of which staked early claims to blockbuster status in their pre-release marketing, that the concept of the Korean blockbuster began to take shape. Chris Berry (2003) argues that in both South Korea and China, filmmakers have attempted to 'de-Westernise' the concept of the blockbuster. In Korea, this has manifested itself in efforts to produce local versions at the same time that competition with Hollywood and the controversy over the Screen Quota system have resulted in a heightened awareness of the qualities (and especially the 'bigness') of US blockbusters. Nonetheless, the reception of Korean blockbusters by critics, journalists and audiences has been highly ambivalent. Although it is clear that, as Berry asserts, 'the blockbuster is no longer American owned' (2003: 218) Korean filmmakers' appropriation of the blockbuster model would remain a topic of intense debate in the coming decade.

Government support and film investment funds

During his campaign for president, Kim Dae Jung promised to give strong financial and regulatory support to the cultural industries. After being elected, he largely followed through on his pledge: the year 2000 marked the first time that culture accounted for more than 1% of the government's total budget. In the realm of cinema, Kim initiated a vast overhaul and expansion of support policies, most notably with the launch of the Korean Film Council (KOFIC) and the government's encouragement of, and participation in, specialised film investment funds. In the next few years, South Korean support of the film industry would grow to vastly exceed that of any other Asian country.

In previous decades, the government body responsible for carrying out film policy was the Korean Motion Picture Promotion Corporation (KMPPC). Launched in 1973, the KMPPC oversaw a handful of programmes to support local filmmakers; one example was the 'Good Films' competition, launched in the 1980s, in which cash awards were presented to the ten best films of the year, as chosen by a group of journalists and critics. Under the Kim Young Sam administration, the body instituted a loan programme for selected film projects: 17 loans totalling 2.88 billion won in 1994, eleven loans totalling 1.85 billion won in 1995 and 14 loans totalling 2.72 billion won in 1996 (see Yi 2005: 412). More significantly, in November 1997 the KMPPC opened the Seoul Studio Complex (later renamed the Namyangju Studio Complex), which provided filmmakers with professional quality soundstages, recording facilities and other amenities for the first time in decades.

After Kim Dae Jung took office, the KMPPC was restructured as a civilian-run organisation and relaunched in May 1999 as the Korean Film Council. The new body received its funding from the Ministry of Culture and Tourism but was largely independent in drafting and carrying out the nation's film policies. It was headed by a group of ten commissioners, including filmmakers, professors and other figures from the film industry, with one among them chosen as a full-time chair. Its funding was also boosted: by its second year, in 2000, KOFIC's total budget of 69.5 billion won ($61 million) was more than double the highest amount granted to the KMPPC under Kim Young Sam.

Nonetheless, in the first year of its existence KOFIC was witness to an intense power struggle between the film industry's older generation, headed by veteran actress Kim Ji-mi who was serving as a KOFIC commissioner, and younger generation producers and directors who had entered the film industry in the late 1980s. Sharp disagreements arose over the allocation of support funds, culminating in public denunciations, lawsuits and the mass resignation of seven of the ten commissioners. Finally, the government sided with the younger members of the film industry, who assumed control of KOFIC and embarked on a decisive overhaul of Korea's film policies. The successful efforts of younger generation filmmakers to gain control over the drafting of film policy stands as an important milestone in the development of New Korean Cinema.

Support programmes initiated in those years were various, including the first ever grants for short and independent films, the creation of regional media centres ('MediACT') to provide education and equipment rental to amateur filmmakers, production support for art-house and low-budget feature films, loans to commercial feature film projects, support for digital films, the production of subtitled prints of selected features and shorts, an expansion of KOFIC's in-house research division, loans and grants to theatres specialising in art-house cinema, and more (See Davis & Yeh 2008: 21–4).

However, one of the most lasting initiatives of the Kim Dae Jung era was KOFIC's active support of specialised investment funds. In partnership with the state-run Small Business Corporation (SBC), with which it had signed a cooperation agreement in 1998, KOFIC turned to Korea's growing venture capital sector to enlist investors in five- to six-year funds that would devote 50–70% of their capital to film financing. By investing in a slate of films, rather than individual titles, it was hoped that risk could be lessened and spread among the fund's various participants. To sweeten the pot, both KOFIC and the SBC agreed to participate themselves, with the latter taking on a greater share of losses should the funds fail to turn a profit.

From 1998 to the end of 2005, the film industry witnessed the launch of 48 funds worth a combined $535 million. Of this total the SBC contributed $121 million and KOFIC $46 million (see Paquet 2007a). Such efforts played a major role in the expansion and diversification of Korea's film finance sector, with venture capital companies (both independently and in the funds described above) emerging as the film industry's most active investors.

Friend, nostalgia and the new male hero

Julian Stringer notes: 'Some movies are born blockbusters; some achieve blockbuster status; some have blockbuster status thrust upon them' (2003: 10). Kwak Kyung-taek's *Friend* (*Chingu*, 2001) ranks in the final category. Based on the director's own experiences, the film centres around four high school boys whose bonds remain unshakable as they pass through adolescence: hanging out at the roller skating rink, fighting students from rival high schools, dealing with broken families, abusive teachers and economic hardship. Later in life, however, two of the men join rival gangs and the group is torn apart. Released in March 2001, the modestly budgeted film stunned observers by soaring past *Shiri* and *JSA*'s totals to record 8.2

The 1980s re-imagined in the smash hit *Friend* (2001)

million admissions (worth $37.6 million at 2001 exchange rates). *Friend* seemed to contain few of the standard building materials of a blockbuster. Although lead actor Jang Dong-gun would later be recognised as one of the industry's biggest stars, at the time of *Friend*'s release he was not considered an unusually strong box-office draw. Likewise, director Kwak, a New York University graduate, was considered a dubious box-office prospect after the flop of his first two films, *3PM Bathhouse Paradise* (*Eoksutang*, 1996) and *Dr. K* (*Dakteokei*, 1999).

Friend nonetheless introduced two novel elements to Korean cinema, one of which was a richly detailed portrait of Korea's second city Busan. Although the city of 3.7 million had formed the backdrop to other recent films such as firefighting drama *Libera Me* (*Ribera me*, 2000), *Friend* was the first to highlight and even revel in the city's distinctive regional character. This was done visually, with evocative portraits of Busan's crowded streets and fish markets, but even more so linguistically, with a heavy but authentic-feeling use of local dialect and slang. Several memorable lines of dialogue, made up of words that many Koreans were hearing for the first time, became catchphrases in the wake of the film's success. From this point on the highlighting of South Korea's many distinctive dialects became a common feature in many Korean films, particularly comedies.

Friend also stands as one of the first Korean films to recast the experiences of the 1970s and 1980s in a personal and highly nostalgic light. After the Korean New Wave drew to a close in 1996 with the release of *A Petal*, some time passed before directors showed an interest in revisiting the politically charged decades of the 1970s and 1980s (Lee Chang-dong's anguished *Peppermint Candy* being one notable exception). When at last they did, it was through coming-of-age films and nostalgic personal recollections of the era. Romantic comedy *Ditto* (*Donggam*, 2000), scripted by well-known playwright/film director Jang Jin, was the first in this lineage, depicting a time-warp HAM radio correspondence between a woman living in 1979 and a man living in 1999. Although the juxtaposition of the two eras highlighted their political differences, the portrayal of the earlier period was marked by strong overtones of nostalgia.

The first half of *Friend* reconstructed as well as de-politicised the early 1980s. The use of pop music (Robert Palmer's 'Bad Case of Loving You'), iconic imagery of the era (shots of the fumigation truck that accompany the opening credits) and universal tropes of adolescence (teen romance, fistfights) induced viewers to recall their own youth. Being such a phenomenal success, *Friend* helped to kick off a trend of 1980s youth films, with other examples including *My Nike (Mutjima paemilli*, 2002), *Bet on My Disco (Haejeok diseuko wang doeda*, 2002), *Conduct Zero (Pumhaengjero*, 2002), *Mr. Gam's Victory (Syupeoseuta gamsayong*, 2004) and *Bravo My Life (Saranghae malsunssi*, 2005). Virtually all such films highlighted the relative poverty of the earlier era, and some proved more willing than others to reference political issues, directly or indirectly.

Korean filmmakers' depictions of the 1980s only underscored how much Korean cinema had changed since that time. On a different level, this ever-widening gap also manifested itself in the characterisations of film protagonists. In his groundbreaking book *The Remasculinization of Korean Cinema*, Kyung Hyun Kim (2004) argues that while portrayals of women in Korean cinema did not undergo a fundamental change between the 1980s and the present, depictions of men went through a noticeable transformation. The traumas of the 1970s and 1980s, and ordinary citizens' powerlessness in the face of authoritarian rule, were reflected in 1980s cinema in a pervading sense of threatened masculinity. The typical male hero of that era, such as the thin, shy college student Byeong-tae from Bae Chang-ho's smash hit *Whale Hunting*, was characterised by his lack of power, and solicited viewer identification and pity. Such depictions served as a critique and counterpoint to the highly masculinised strain of nationalism pushed by the military regime, though Kim argues that in structuring many narratives around the quest and ultimate attainment of masculine power, such films ended up reaffirming the status quo. Other male protagonists, from the angry young men of *Fine Windy Day* and *Chilsu and Mansu*, to the intellectual writers in *White Badge, To You, From Me* and *A Single Spark*, also grapple with the aftermath of trauma and seek release from anxiety.

The industrialised, global age of the early 2000s produced a new kind of male hero, as epitomised by the sleek, muscled protagonists of *Friend* played by Jang Dong-gun and Yoo Oh-sung. Freed of anxiety and fear, the self-confident, articulate men of New Korean Cinema emerged as objects of desire. And yet there also lay within these characterisations a new capacity for aggression and sadism. Such idealised heroes were, in Kim's words, 'confidently violent' (2004: 232).

High concept comedies and the 50% market share

With the triumphant success of *Shiri*, *JSA* and then *Friend*, venture capital companies were soon clamouring for more big-budget, genre orientated projects in which to invest. However, the next few years would not be kind to the Korean blockbuster. A string of expensive genre films including futuristic action movie *Yesterday* (*Yeseuteotei*, 2002), family adventure *R U Ready?* (*A yu redi?*, 2002), subway-set action film *Tube* (*Tyubeu*, 2003), science fiction feature *Natural City* (*Naechyureol siti*, 2003) and most spectacularly Jang Sun-woo's fascinating but commercially disastrous cyber action film *Resurrection of the Little Match Girl* all flopped at the box office, putting their investors deeply into debt. Such titles were marketed on the basis of their genre credentials, high budgets and advanced special effects. Nonetheless, they were not as localised as *Shiri* and *JSA*, which, in retrospect, may have contributed to their undoing: all of the above films lacked A-list stars and did not engage significantly with local issues. Notably, the one commercially successful (if critically lambasted) blockbuster of 2002, sci-fi action film *2009 Lost Memories* (*2009 roseuteu memorijeu*, 2002), featured top star Jang Dong-gun and a plot focused on Japanese-Korean relations. Set in an alternate future, it imagined that Korea had remained a colony of Japan into the early twenty-first century.

Meanwhile, another kind of film was rapidly gaining popularity among viewers. The high concept comedy, targeted at youth audiences and featuring an easy to describe central premise, had been gaining momentum since the breakout hit *Attack the Gas Station!* (*Juyuso seupgyeok sageon*) in 1999. Directed by Kim Sang-jin, the film depicted four rowdy young hooligans who rob a gas station and, finding no money in the cash register, decide to take the staff hostage and pump gas all night, keeping the proceeds for themselves ('This is a cash and full-tank only day', they inform puzzled customers). Shot on a single set, the film draws its laughs from the way that power relations shift among the various characters who show up on that chaotic night. Key to the film's sensibility is the reason given by the four protagonists for robbing the station in the first place: *'geunyang'*, translatable as 'just because' or 'just for the hell of it'.

Nancy Abelmann and Jung-ah Choi (2005) argue that the word *geunyang* in this context works as a rejection of coherent narration, in keeping with the film's romanticised anti-establishment attitude – but is also linked to broader social transformations in the 1990s. Under authoritarian rule, South Korea had been dominated by grand narratives ('development' and 'anti-communism' at one end of the political spectrum; at the other, 'anti-state activism'), which demanded subordination of the personal for the greater good. In the 1990s, grand narratives began to lose much of their pull, and a backlash arose against this type of collective logic. The carefree, self-directed and somewhat callous attitude behind the word *geunyang* was thus 'emblematic of changed times' (2005: 134).

A similar mindset underwrites the most popular sub-genre to emerge in the early 2000s: the gangster comedy. Although the influential *No. 3* (*Neombeo 3*, 1997) served as an important model, the gangster comedy came into its own in the second half of 2001 with a string of runaway hits including *Kick the Moon* (*Sillaui dalbam*) (4.4 million nationwide admissions), *My Wife Is a Gangster* (*Jopong manura*) (5.2 million), *Hi Dharma* (*Dalmaya nolja*) (3.7 million) and *My Boss, My Hero* (*Dusabuilche*) (3.3 million). Whereas *Friend* had portrayed the world of organised crime in a sombre and almost reverential light, the gangsters who populate the comedies display a pugnacious, self-centred impudence that becomes an open target for ridicule. Needless to say, they feel no compulsion to subordinate the personal for the greater good – quite the opposite. However, the directors of these films often juxtapose the behaviour of the gangsters with that of authority figures in Korean society. In Kim Sang-jin's *Kick the Moon*, a gangster and a high school physical education teacher compete for the attentions of a beautiful woman, and in the process the teacher is shown to be the more thug-like personality. In *My Boss, My Hero*, a dim-witted middle-ranking gangster is sent back to high school by his boss to earn his diploma; however, he soon discovers that the school administration is corrupt on a grand scale, leading to an ironic final showdown between school officials and organised criminals who fight to restore fairness to the educational system. In *Hi Dharma*, a group of gangsters forced into hiding demand refuge at a remote Buddhist monastery. This time it is the monks who set the moral example for the gangsters, but not before the former prove to be just as skilled at fighting as the latter.

The most commercially successful film of the group was Jo Hyun-jin's *My Wife Is a Gangster*, starring actress Shin Eun-kyung as a ruthless crime boss who is persuaded by her terminally ill sister to find a husband. Eventually settling on a naive government clerk who suspects nothing about her true profession, she marries and continues her criminal activities in secret until an unexpected pregnancy ensues. Juxtaposing middle-class family life and the more sensational life of a gang leader, the film undercuts stereotypes and traditional gender roles in a teasingly provocative manner before (continuing a long tradition in Korean comedy) reasserting patriarchal values in its final reel.

The runaway success of *Friend* and the gangster comedy helped Korean cinema to capture an unprecedented 50.1% market share in 2001. Three years earlier, even a 40% market share had seemed impossibly out of reach, so this achievement had a profound psychological effect on the industry.

Significantly, producers had found box-office success with not one but several different filmmaking models. Film magazine *Cine21* observed that the more commercial projects that were driving the development of New Korean Cinema fell into three broad categories. The first, the producer-orientated project, including the high concept comedies mentioned above, were typically built around a catchy central premise and shot with mid-level stars. Less expensive than the other two categories, they cost an average of $2 million to produce and were shot in three to four months. Other prominent examples include *Sex Is Zero* (*Saekjeuksigong*, 2002), a sex comedy set in a university, and *Marrying the Mafia* (*Gamunui yeonggwang*, 2002), about a gangster family who plot to marry off their daughter to a young lawyer.

In contrast, director-orientated projects were built around a well-developed screenplay and a director's authorial style. More expensive to make ($3 million on average), they employed highly experienced crew members and big-name stars, who often preferred working on projects that tested their acting abilities. Director-orientated projects included infidelity drama *Happy End* (*Haepi endeu*, 1999) and Park Chan-wook's follow-up to *JSA*, *Sympathy for Mr. Vengeance* (*Boksuneun naui geot*, 2002). The third category was the Korean blockbuster, which cost about $6 million to make, much of it spent on *mise-en-scène* and special effects. As noted above, at this time many producers felt that A-list stars would not be necessary to attract viewers, who would instead be drawn by the film's effects and technical qualities. In later years, however, stars would come to be seen as an essential part of the blockbuster package.

Throughout the commercial boom years of 1999 to 2006, each of these three commercial models would experience rises and falls in fortune. In 2001 and 2002, Korean critics began to lament the success of producer-orientated projects at the expense of director-orientated cinema, and worried aloud that investors would shift the vast majority of their funds to the former. However, as noted in the next chapter, director-orientated projects staged an eye-opening commercial comeback in 2003, just as high concept comedies began to struggle. Similarly, many pundits were ready to announce the death of the Korean blockbuster in 2003, but later events would prove them wrong. The unpredictable nature of viewers' tastes in the first decade of the twenty-first century went a long way towards ensuring that no one model of production became dominant, with positive results for the overall diversity of Korean cinema.

Meanwhile, dramatic developments in commercial film did not mean that auteur cinema was dead. Some of the names best associated with New Korean Cinema occupy a space that is partially removed and partially connected with the movement's dominant trends. One hesitates to distinguish unilaterally between art-house and commercial cinema in any aesthetic or qualitative sense, since on closer analysis such distinctions usually rest on unstable foundations. It is also worth noting that art-house films sometimes have real box-office clout: *Oasis* (*Oasiseu*), the third film by director Lee Chang-dong, spent three weeks at number one at the box office in autumn 2002. However, the works of Hong Sang-soo, Lee Chang-dong and Kim Ki-duk, among many others, spring from a different model of production from those described above, and given the strong individual character of their films they will be considered separately below.

New auteurs: Hong Sang-soo

The debut of Hong Sang-soo in May 1996 with *The Day a Pig Fell into the Well* (*Dwaejiga umure ppajin nal*) was, as described in film magazine *Cine21*, 'a gunshot that shook Korean film history' (quoted in Huh 2007a: 3). Told in four segments, each focusing on a different character (a frustrated novelist, his married lover, her timid husband and a ticket vendor in love with the novelist), the film was made of languid, everyday scenes but it was the manner in which they were shot and presented that drew notice. On one level, Hong's sensitivity to behaviour and gift for language imparted to even the simplest exchanges between characters a vivid (or, perhaps, an enhanced) realism. At the same time the camera's objective viewpoint and the director's refusal to emphasise any one aspect of the image or story over another left viewers labouring to construct meaning out of what they saw. Finally, and somewhat surprisingly, when viewers stepped back to consider the film as a whole they discovered a complex interlocking structure in which details and lines of dialogue from one part of the film, which may have initially seemed unimportant, echoed and reinforced those from another. According to film critic Huh Moonyung, 'The cinematic language spoken in this film was unprecedented in Korean film history. Korean movie critics thought of names like Robert Bresson and Luis Buñuel, but they agonised over the genealogy of a movie that was completely unique' (2007a: 3). Hong's cinematic style would emerge in clearer terms in his subsequent films, yet in some ways the puzzle remained. Although not granted the international recognition of Asia's most famous auteurs, his works display a level of originality that demand, and sometimes elude, explanation.

David Bordwell argues that Hong's films fit broadly into the minimalist tradition taken up by Asian filmmakers such as Hou Hsiao-hsien, Tsai Ming-liang and Kore-eda Hirokazu, in adopting episodic rather than goalorientated narratives; in focusing on mundane, everyday occurrences; and in omitting important scenes or background information, leaving viewers unsure about characters' motivations. Visually as well, Hong shares with Asian minimalist films an austerity in camerawork that forces the viewer to focus on small details. However, Bordwell argues that Hong 'has developed a strikingly original approach to overall narrative architecture' (2007: 22).

Hong's first three films in particular adopt an almost geometric approach to narrative. *The Power of Kangwon Province* (*Gangwondoui him*, 1998), structured in two major parts, initially focuses on Jisuk (Oh Yoonhong), a woman who travels to the east coast of Korea with her friends after breaking up with a married university instructor named Sang-gwon (Baek Jong-hak). The second part centres on Sang-gwon, who, without realising it and unbeknownst to Jisuk, takes the same train to Kangwon Province and passes time in the same locations, though they never meet. Hong, who in interviews has referred to this story of separated lovers as a (2-1)+(2-1)=2 structure (quoted in Huh 2007b: 54), complicates the relationship by playing with time (for example, by showing Jisuk erasing some graffiti off a wall, and then later in the film presenting the scene when Sang-gwon wrote it), and by withholding information so that we do not realise that Sang-gwon is Jisuk's former lover until the film's final reel.

The relationship between two major narrative segments is even more complex in *Virgin Stripped Bare by Her Bachelors* (*O! sujeong*, 2000). This film, shot in black-and-white, juxtaposes two extended flashbacks: one seemingly based on the memories or perspective of Jae-hun (Jung Bo-seok), a wealthy single man; and another on the perspective of Su-jeong (Lee Eun-ju), who meets him by chance and gradually acquiesces to his sexual advances. Significantly, the two flashbacks often overlap so that we see the same scene presented twice, each time subtly different. The personality of each character also varies in each segment, filtered through the lenses of selective memory and ego. And yet the segments are not shot strictly according to point of view: some of the scenes presented could not have been witnessed by the character in question, and ultimately the nature of the flashbacks remains unclear. Hong also includes three scenes that take place in the present, placed at the beginning, the middle and the end of the film.

Beginning with his fourth film *Turning Gate* (*Saenghwarui balkkyeon*, 2002) Hong's narratives have followed more familiar, chronological patterns of development. Yet they remain just as complex, with their echoes and repetitions expressed in the work's details, rather than unusual narrative structures. Astute viewers may also notice links between different films. As Bordwell notes, 'the later films tease us with the possibility that at any moment we will swerve into an echo chamber' (2007: 28).

Hong, who studied at the California College of Arts and Crafts and the Art Institute of Chicago, has adopted an unusual approach to shooting that favours intuition and on-site inspiration over planning out scenes in advance. Working from a detailed treatment rather than a script, he writes out the dialogue for each scene on the set, on the morning of the day it is to be shot. Similarly, camera placement and angles are decided not in advance but on the set in consultation with the cinematographer. Hong works closely with his cast in developing each character, yet at the moment of shooting he does not solicit improvisation, giving his actors very precise instructions down to the smallest details and inflections.

This may account for the fact that the complex patterns that emerge in his works seem to replicate psychological rather than abstract or physical structures. Hong claims that vague feelings or unconscious preferences

A suicide initiates a travel back through 20 years of Korean history in Lee Chang-dong's *Peppermint Candy* (2000)

serve as the basis for many of the elements in his films. He explains: 'I do calculate, but the decisions are made by intuition. It is easy to calculate once the structure is set. It's intuition that decides where to draw the line' (quoted in Huh 2007b: 59).

New auteurs: Lee Chang-dong

As the world celebrated on the night of 31 December 1999, die-hard Korean cinephiles marked the start of the new millennium in a different way. As the clock struck midnight, Lee Chang-dong's second film *Peppermint Candy* officially launched its commercial release with a late-night screening. Although far from celebratory in its content, the film was nonetheless a fitting observation of Korea's move into the twenty-first century.

Inspired by the Harold Pinter play *Betrayal* (1978), Lee's film is told in reverse chronological order, progressing backwards through the life of its protagonist, but also (in both symbolic and literal fashion) revisiting two decades in recent Korean history. The first chapter, titled 'Outdoor Excursion, 1999', introduces us to the protagonist Yeong-ho (Sul Kyung-gu), a man in a crumpled suit who turns up unexpectedly at a riverside reunion of former factory workers. Yeong-ho frightens everyone with his crazed and erratic behaviour, then clambers up onto a railroad bridge. One concerned man pleads with him to come down, but Yeong-ho throws himself in front of an oncoming train, shouting, 'I want to go back!' – a phrase that will resonate throughout the film. The next chapter takes place three days before the suicide, with Yeong-ho buying a gun and then visiting a hospital to see a woman in a coma. Chapter three presents Yeong-ho as a small business owner in summer 1994, though we know from a line of dialogue in the previous chapter that his venture will end in financial ruin. Chapter four shows him as a police detective torturing student dissidents in spring 1987; a scene where he dunks a man's head in the water recalls the death of Park Jong-cheol, which helped spark the massive protests that year. In chapter five, set in autumn 1984, he is a new recruit to the police force. Chapter six sees him as a military conscript in May 1980, when he finds himself sent with his fellow soldiers on an assignment to Gwangju to suppress the popular uprising. The final chapter depicts a picnic in autumn 1979 alongside the same river which opened the film. Meanwhile, in between each chapter is a brief insert, shot from the perspective of a running train and presented in reverse – the receding figures suggest a trip backwards in time.

As noted by Hye Seung Chung and David Scott Diffrient (2007), *Peppermint Candy*'s unusual narrative structure derives its power from the contrast between the implied chronological chain of events (the story, or in Russian formalist terms the *fabula* – progressing from 1979 to 1999), and the arrangement of the story in cinematic time (the plot or *syuzhet,* moving from 1999 to 1979). As a result, many of the objects, actions or lines of dialogue encountered in the film – such as a camera which seems to make Yeong-ho uncomfortable, the comment 'life is beautiful' and a jar of peppermint candies – appear initially to the viewer as riddles or enigmas, before they are given deeper meaning in subsequent chapters. Chung and Diffrient contend that the ultimate effect of this is not the shock of surprise we associate with the revelation of mysteries, but a sense of bitter irony. In this film, knowledge of the future only makes the past more painful to watch.

Now canonised as a modern classic, *Peppermint Candy* confirmed the promise shown by Lee in his debut film *Green Fish* (*Chorogmulgogi*, 1997), about a man in a quickly developing suburb of Seoul who seeks employment and purpose in organised crime. As a director Lee has become known for confronting sensitive topics in an austere, rigorous manner. He says, 'Some audiences complain that my films are so tightly knit together and intentional that there is no place for them to escape. I admit this is true, but I don't think it's something I should avoid. If a film is to capture an audience, then [having] no way of escape is a virtue' (quoted in Kim Young-jin 2007a: 66). His third film *Oasis*, which won a best director award at the

Venice Film Festival, depicts a love affair between an ex-convict, Jong-du (Sul Kyung-gu) and Gong-ju (Moon So-ri), a woman with severe cerebral palsy. In its form, the film resembled a traditional melodrama, with two lovers struggling to maintain their relationship in a hostile world, but Lee's austere style denied viewers any usual sense of emotional release. Although less epic in scope than *Peppermint Candy*, *Oasis* ranks as one of his strongest works, never romanticising the protagonists' plight but depicting the neglect and discrimination they receive with a sober intensity. The outstanding, absolutely convincing performances Lee coaxed from his lead actors Sul and Moon were particularly notable.

Lee, who began his career as a successful novelist, took an unusual detour in early 2003. At the request of newly elected president Roh Moo Hyun, he took up the position of Minister of Culture and Tourism – the first film director in Korea ever to do so. His appointment was greeted with wide expectation, though ultimately his ambition to bring about lasting change in the nation's cultural policies would become mired in political deadlock. Lee's return to filmmaking after his resignation in mid-2004 was *Secret Sunshine* (*Miryang*, 2007), based on a short story about a woman who turns to religion after her son is kidnapped. The acclaimed work was invited to the Cannes Film Festival where the film's lead, Jeon Do-yeon, one of Korea's most talented performers, was presented with a Best Actress award for her performance. Lee's bleakest and most emotionally devastating film to date, *Secret Sunshine* appears at first to be taking aim at the excesses of Korean Christian groups, but it ultimately becomes more focused on abstract, philosophical questions (and Lee himself denies any anti-religious agenda). The film is in some ways like a twenty-first-century, cinematic version of a Matthew Arnold poem, pondering the emptiness of a world where religion has lost its legitimacy. However, while the beauty of Arnold's language and imagery act as a kind of salve to his readers, Lee's tightly-bound filmic style offers no such consolation.

New auteurs: Kim Ki-duk

Director Kim Ki-duk entered the industry as an outsider, and although he has been supported in his rise to prominence by the Pusan International Film Festival, the Korean Film Council and local distributors/investors such as Sponge Entertainment, he remains in many ways removed from dominant trends in Korean cinema. Born in 1960 in the village of Bonghwa in North Gyeongsang Province, Kim dropped out of high school and spent his twenties serving in the marines, working in factories and volunteering at a church for the visually impaired. Having long pursued painting as a hobby, in 1990 he flew to Paris and spent two years selling his paintings on the street. Kim says it was at this time that he went to a movie theatre for the first time in his life.

After returning to Korea, Kim won a government-sponsored screenplay contest and then made his debut with *Crocodile* (*Ageo*, 1996), a crudely directed but visually inventive film about a man who fishes the bodies of suicides out of the Han River in Seoul and holds them for ransom. The director's early works, including the Paris-set *Wild Animals* (*Yasaengdongmul bohoguyeok*, 1997) and *Birdcage Inn* (*Paran daemun*, 1998), focus on marginalised characters at the bottom of the social ladder, of a completely different sort than those evoked by the term *minjung*: pimps, low-ranking gangsters, prostitutes. Imbued with strong violence and a predatory sexuality, Kim's narratives displayed a visceral feel for cruelty and class conflict. Cédric Lagandré observes: 'People don't talk to each other in Kim Ki-duk's films, people hit each other. Relationships are always frontal, direct, decoded, never mediated through language which would neutralise the violence and allow individualities to meet in the neutrality of a shared space' (2006: 60). Neither local viewers nor critics warmed to Kim's early films. Feminists in particular were enraged at the lack of agency granted to female characters in his films, calling him a 'monster', a 'psycho' and a 'good-for-nothing filmmaker' (quoted in Lee 2001).

Controversy surrounds several of his best-known works from this period. *The Isle* (2000) takes place on a remote lake dotted with floating cabins where lodgers sleep, fish and buy sex from the reclusive woman, Hee-jin (Suh Jung), who serves them. One of her customers, Hyun-shik (Kim Yu-seok) is on the run from the police after killing his lover. After Hee-jin stops him from committing suicide, the two enter into a wordless but intense sexual relationship marked by sudden bursts of violence and self-mutilation. One particularly gruesome scene involving fish hooks caused an Italian journalist to faint during the official screening at the Venice Film Festival. The film creates a vivid sense of space, and is also a primary example of Kim's curiously unconcerned approach to traditional character development. Many of the characters in his films seem to act not according to their own internal dynamics, but to satisfy the broader aims of the film. When, on the set, actress Suh Jung accused him of affording less importance to her character than to the dog that appears in the film, Kim replied that no, he considered her character to be on an equal footing with the dog – but to be less important than the boat she rows (see Lee 2001). *Bad Guy (Nappeun namja*, 2002) is about a pimp who abducts a university student and forces her into prostitution. Although registering the full scale of the horror visited upon the woman, the film also increasingly sides with its male hero, who has fallen in love with her. By the film's end they are travelling the country and practising prostitution from the back of a truck: an ostensibly happy ending. While not apologising for the unethical behaviour or misogyny portrayed in Kim's films, Steve Choe argues that their circulation through the international film festival circuit served to produce a crisis around the very issue of ethics. Such filmmaking, he notes, 'seems to unsettle liberal tastes with images that violently force viewers to reconsider their familiar modes of cinema going' (2007: 69).

Kim shifted into a more reflective, less controversial mode in 2003 to 2004, when he began basing his films on such themes as redemption and forgiveness. *Spring, Summer, Fall, Winter … and Spring (Bom yeoreum gaeul gyeoul geurigo bom*, 2003) is set on a remote lake and depicts progressive stages in the life of a Buddhist monk. Although not, as it sometimes appears to be, a film grounded in actual Buddhist doctrine, it showcased Kim's visual creativity and his ability to tell stories with a bare minimum of dialogue. At its premiere at the Locarno International Film Festival the film was afforded breathless praise by many critics and enjoyed subsequent commercial success in Germany, Spain, the US and other territories.

The following year would see Kim win two high-profile festival awards: a best director award from the Berlin International Film Festival in February for *Samaritan Girl (Samaria*, 2004) and another best director award from the Venice Film Festival in September for *3-Iron (Bin jip*, 2004). Both films were shot in the space of roughly two weeks on minimal budgets, funded almost entirely by pre-sales to foreign countries. *3-Iron* in particular gained a reputation as one of Kim's strongest works. Tae-suk (Jae Hee) is a man who lives his life breaking into empty houses, living there for a time (sometimes fixing broken appliances) and then departing, leaving everything in its place. In one home he comes across a woman named Sun-hwa (Lee Seung-yun) who suffers from marital abuse, and the two set off together to live their curious, alternative lifestyle. The simple and almost wordless story is in part a philosophy of living, with its critique of the idea of possession (both of physical objects and the husband's possessive desire for his wife). In the film's abstract final act, viewers begin to question whether the characters even exist, or if they are disembodied spirits, but Kim's imagery is suggestive enough to support multiple interpretations.

Kim's festival accolades and overseas success have turned him into a household name in Korea; nonetheless, his works have largely failed to find commercial success at home. His relationship with the local press and audience reached a low point in 2006 before the release of his thirteenth film *Time* (*Sigan*). Bemoaning Korean viewers' lack of interest in art-house cinema, Kim vowed not to release any more of his films domestically if *Time* failed to sell 300,000 tickets. Although ultimately retracting his threat (the film sold just over 28,000 tickets), the incident highlighted the at-times wide gap between the domestic reception of Korean films and their commercial and critical reputation abroad.

4   NEW AMBITIONS

South Korea co-hosted the football World Cup together with Japan in June 2002. It had been 14 years since the Seoul Olympics, which the nation's military leaders had billed as a mark of Korea's entry into the ranks of developed nations. By 2002, the country boasted the world's eleventh largest economy despite a comparatively small population of 49 million people, and was considered a technological leader in the fields of broadband, mobile telecommunications and electronics. Nonetheless, many Koreans felt their culture and achievements to be under-recognised internationally. The World Cup provided South Korea with an opportunity to present images of a modern, dynamic society to viewers around the globe. When the national team made an unprecedented entry into the tournament's semi-finals, it provided hope that on some level this aim had been reached.

News of other unexpected achievements in the fields of business, sports, science and technology appeared in the middle part of the decade. In 2005, Samsung passed Sony to become the world's largest electronics company, and the following year its revenue exceeded the GDP of Argentina. Korean scientists also made a number of high profile advances in the field of biotechnology – though revelations at the end of 2005 that top researcher Hwang Woo-suk had used faked data in his studies affected the celebratory mood.

The most unexpected successes of all came in the fields of music, television and cinema. For several years it had been apparent that Korean pop culture was winning over a significant fan base in other parts of Asia. Television footage of Korean singers or TV stars being chased by crowds of adoring fans in China and Vietnam elicited a stunned response from Korean viewers in the late 1990s, given that local films and television dramas had never before provoked much interest among young Asian consumers. However, by the mid-2000s such scenes had become commonplace and journalists across the continent were proclaiming Korean pop culture the hot new thing. Dubbed *hallyu* or the 'Korean Wave' (not to be confused with the Korean New Wave), this grassroots enthusiasm for all things Korean would transform the nation's image throughout Asia. From Singapore to Hong Kong, enrolment in Korean language classes shot up, while in Japan, long-standing prejudice against Koreans began to be tempered by the phenomenal popularity of *hallyu* stars. Tourism surged, with locations from famous films and television dramas drawing especially large numbers of visitors. Back in the 1990s, government officials in Korea had recognised the potential for cinema as an industry. In the 2000s, they began to understand that the spread of cultural contents could have a much broader impact than the export of automobiles and flatscreen televisions.

Meanwhile, on the political stage, the election at the end of 2002 to replace Kim Dae Jung had produced another president from the progressive camp, a human rights lawyer turned politician named Roh Moo Hyun. Roh's campaign had enjoyed high-profile support from several film industry figures, including actor Moon Sung-keun (*A Petal*), producer Myung Kay-nam (*Peppermint Candy*) and director Lee Chang-dong, who as noted earlier was chosen by the new president to lead the Ministry of Culture and Tourism. Roh would mostly continue the policies of his predecessor with regards to the film industry, providing generous levels of financial support. However, his presidency in general, having initially drawn forth tremendous expectations from young and left-leaning voters, soon lost momentum amidst controversy and political deadlock.

Commercial auteurs: Park Chan-wook, Bong Joon-ho, Kim Jee-woon

The development of *hallyu* or the Korean Wave, to be discussed further below, was shaped to a large degree by the Korean star system. At the same time, however, a group of directors were establishing names for themselves with ambitious works that won praise at international film

Song Kang-ho in Bong
Joon-ho's *Memories of
Murder* (2003)

festivals and emerged as high-grossing event films at home. Such 'commercial auteurs' as Kim Jee-woon, Park Chan-wook and Bong Joon-ho were
able to create films of a highly distinctive character within the confines of
the mainstream industry, and they are responsible for giving New Korean
Cinema some of its most memorable films.

The year 2003 marked a key breakthrough for each of the three directors mentioned above. In April, director Bong Joon-ho released his second
film *Memories of Murder*, based on a real-life incident in the 1980s in
which a serial killer eluded investigators and terrorised the residents of
a rural town. Although adopting the form of a police procedural, the film
establishes its independence from genre conventions with its abrupt shifts
in mood, dark humour and its undermining of audience sympathies and
expectations. Bong's cinephile roots are evident in an early sequence in
which police detectives arrive at a crime scene where a new body has been
discovered. The chaos of the moment and the ineffectiveness of the police
force are captured in a meandering, richly choreographed single take that
recalls other classic uses of the technique such as the opening of Orson
Welles' *Touch of Evil* (1958).

The film also provides vivid illustration of the workings of society under
authoritarian rule. The casual manner in which local detectives beat con-
fessions out of their suspects is representative of a mindset that reaches to
the top of the government. Bong shows how such practices ultimately come
back to weaken the system and hinder the investigation. At the same time,
the film demonstrates directly how a government so focused on controlling
and suppressing its populace is ultimately unable to protect them.

Midway through the film, a detective from Seoul arrives in the town and begins pursuing a more enlightened, deductive-based approach to solving the crimes. Yet this too proves powerless to stop the murderer, who functions in this work as a kind of force of pure malevolence. Despite the film's similarities to the mystery genre, it ultimately pursues opposite ends. The average mystery develops by empowering its hero and the viewer with increased knowledge. However, particularly in the film's enigmatic climax, *Memories of Murder* forces viewers to confront their own inability to solve or fully understand the case, and thus leads them to question even their most basic assumptions.

Memories of Murder won immediate critical and popular acclaim on its release, and its box-office take of over five million admissions not only established Bong as a leading filmmaker, but also demonstrated the commercial potential of such highly individualistic, director-orientated films. Soon local journalists were proclaiming 'well-made' (transliterated from English) to be the newest industry buzzword. Kim So-hui (2004), editor of film magazine *Cine21*, described 'well-made' in this context as a commercial feature that makes use of defined genres and the star system, but which contains both a distinctive directorial style and commentary on social issues.

Another 'well-made' film opened in June: Kim Jee-woon's horror film *A Tale of Two Sisters (Janghwa, hongnyeon*, 2003). Loosely based on a Korean folk tale, the film focuses on an adolescent girl who returns from a sanitarium to live with her father, stepmother and younger sister in an isolated country cottage. At first the narrative seems to focus on the younger sister Su-yeon's (Moon Geun-young) nightmares, the eerie atmosphere in the home (where there seems to be a ghost) and a growing tension between the older sister Su-mi (Lim Soo-jung) and the stepmother, Eun-ju (Yum Jung-ah). Yet the plot takes several sharp turns as it becomes apparent that Su-mi, suffering from trauma and guilt, has created some of the personalities that live within her psychological world. Daringly complex for such a commercial project, the film invites all manner of psychoanalytic interpretation at the same time as it can be enjoyed on the surface as a visually sumptuous and terrifying story. Critic Kim Hyung-seok labels the film as 'subversive horror' in the sense that rather than staging a confrontation between the subject and the other, *A Tale of Two Sisters* ultimately locates the other within the subject (2008: 65). The outside world turns out to be far less threatening than the horror that exists within the mind itself.

It is also a primary example of the manner in which Kim prioritises the visual over narrative, foregrounding repeated images, symbolic actions (like the washing of hands) and the predominance of facial close-ups. The director says: 'I had hidden so much of the theme and story within the picture that the story had to be simple. If you're doing a hidden picture puzzle, where's the fun if you only look at the picture on the surface and don't look for the hidden images?' (quoted in Kim Hyung-seok 2008: 113). Despite the film's unconventional touches it sold over three million tickets and remains to this day the highest grossing horror movie in Korean film history.

Finally one of the iconic works of New Korean Cinema, Park Chan-wook's *Oldboy*, was released in November. Based loosely on a Japanese *manga*, the film revolves around the character of Oh Dae-soo, who spends 15 years in a bizarre privately-run jail without ever being informed of his crime. One day he is released, waking up at the top of a building wearing a new suit. He is soon contacted by the mysterious Lee Woo-jin (Yoo Ji-tae), who challenges him to discover within five days the reason for his imprisonment. However, Oh is primarily concerned with vengeance. From this point on, it is his rage and determination that gives the film its powerful momentum – accomplished cinematically with Park's inventive filmmaking and the visceral performance of lead actor Choi Min-sik.

On one level, *Oldboy* is an expression of pure cinematic revelry. Drawing inspiration from Alfred Hitchcock, Brian De Palma and other filmmakers, Park makes use of a wide array of cinematic techniques to create some of the most striking, memorable images in Korean cinema. Much of this has to do with the director's use of the camera as an active, constantly moving presence. Shifting suddenly from one perspective to the other, from extreme close-ups to birds-eye views to straight-on medium shots with the character facing the lens, Park replicates on an emotional level the protagonist's desperate hunt for his adversary. Key actions are also frequently omitted. For example, viewers see Dae-soo lying on the floor of his cell surrounded by broken glass and with blood stains on the rug near his head, but do not witness him hit his head into the mirror. In being made to piece together such fleeting elisions themselves, viewers are pulled into the narrative's relentless progression. One of the film's most famous scenes is a one man vs twenty fight sequence in a hallway.

Originally conceived in the film's storyboard in over forty separate shots, it was ultimately rendered in a single take. In contrast to the chaotic jumble of bodies and the swinging of hammers and sticks, the movement of the camera is a model of simplicity: held in long shot, it merely tracks left and right to keep the protagonist in the middle of the screen. In other scenes Park makes use of sudden fantasy sequences, as when the film's female lead Mido (Gang Hye-jung), after proclaiming that very lonely people keep seeing ants, imagines a human-sized ant on an empty subway train. Meanwhile, the use of saturated colours, stylish set design (like *A Tale of Two Sisters*, wallpaper of fantastic patterns keeps reappearing in *Oldboy*), and curious archaic-sounding dialogue combine to create a wholly original feel to the film.

Beneath the film's seductive filmmaking lies a dark sensibility and a surprisingly sober contemplation of such issues as sin and vengeance. Although in Western countries much of the discourse surrounding the film has focused on its elemental violence (including a severed tongue, no less disturbing for not being shown onscreen; and Oh Dae-soo biting into a live octopus), there is little of the tongue-in-cheek mischief that characterises scenes of graphic violence in, for example, the works of Quentin Tarantino. Park has stated that his intention in shooting the films in his so-called vengeance trilogy (including also *Sympathy for Mr. Vengeance* from 2002 and *Lady Vengeance* (*Chinjeolhan Geumjassi*) from 2005) was to show the ultimate futility and emptiness of revenge. In *Oldboy* especially, Park presents his characters as archetypal figures, lending the work something of the qualities of an ancient myth or fairytale.

Despite its dark themes, *Oldboy* emerged as a major hit on its local release (3.3 million admissions). Then in May 2004 it was invited to screen in competition at the Cannes Film Festival, where a jury headed by Quentin Tarantino awarded it the Grand Jury prize – the festival's second highest honour. It was the most prestigious award Korean cinema had ever received, and it helped to turn Park and other top Korean directors into household names at home. Such fame would increasingly translate into virtually total creative control over their films.

Interestingly, there is one actor who has played an integral part in the filmographies of all three of the above-mentioned directors. Born in 1967, Song Kang-ho started his career in the theatre before appearing in a small role in Hong Sang-soo's *The Day a Pig Fell into the Well*. He first drew mainstream attention playing a hapless gangster engaged in training three recruits in the comedy *No.3*. Although Song receives only limited screen time, one scene in particular when he disciplines his recruits is recognised as one of the standout comedic performances in Korean film history. After appearing in key supporting roles in Kim Jee-woon's *The Quiet Family* and blockbuster *Shiri,* he took the lead in Kim's second film *The Foul King* (*Banchikwang*, 2000), about a shy businessman who takes up WWF-style pro-wrestling in secret. It was in this performance, which encompassed everything from acrobatic stunts in the wrestling ring to abject humiliation in the office, that Song first displayed the emotional depth that would characterise his later roles.

He went on to work with Park Chan-wook (*JSA, Sympathy for Mr. Vengeance, Thirst* (*Bakchwi*, 2009)), Bong Joon-ho (*Memories of Murder, The Host* (*Goemul*, 2006)) and Kim Jee-woon (*The Good, the Bad, the Weird* (*Joeunnom nappeunnom isanghannom*, 2008)) not to mention Lee Chang-dong (*Secret Sunshine*) and several debut directors, to amass the most remarkable filmography of any Korean actor of the last decade. His contribution to such works, through the theatricality of his body movements and the unusual expressiveness of his voice, should not be overlooked. Although Asian viewers may recall good-looking young stars at the mention of the words 'Korean film', in Europe and North America the most representative image of this national cinema may be that of Song Kang-ho's inscrutable face.

Ten million admissions

Although by mid-2003 many industry observers had written off big-budget genre fare as overly risky and commercially dubious, the Korean blockbuster would stage a furious comeback at the end of the year with *Silmido* (*Silmido*, 2003) and *Tae Guk Gi* (*Taegeukki hwinallimyeo*, 2004), the first Korean films ever to sell more than ten million tickets. Directed by Kang Woo-suk – founder of distributor Cinema Service, director of hit films *Two Cops* (*Tukapsseu*, 1993) and *Public Enemy* (*Gonggongui jeok*, 2002), and voted nine years in a row the most powerful figure in the Korean film industry – *Silmido* is based on a real-life incident in the late 1960s when a group of men were abducted by the government and then trained under extremely harsh conditions to infiltrate North Korea, with the goal of assassinating leader Kim Il-sung. When in the early 1970s a period of detente set in between the North and South, the men were abandoned and they responded by hijacking a bus and setting off for the president's office. Adapted for the screen in bombastic, melodramatic style, the film, with its 8.4 billion won ($7.3 million) budget, received wide publicity when the local media began to look back on the almost-forgotten incident and interview family members of the deceased men. On 19 February 2004, less than two months after its release, *Silmido* became the first Korean film ever to pass the ten million admissions mark. It would end its run with 11.2 million tickets sold. Observers were shocked that a single film could sell so many tickets in a country with a population of 49 million. Although *Silmido* did not go on to perform well internationally, its domestic success would re-focus attention on the film industry and inspire similarly large-scale, commercial films based on recent history such as *May 18* (2007). The traumas of Korea's turbulent twentieth century, which were still visible under the surface of contemporary society, had proved to be rich source material for commercial cinema.

Tae Guk Gi is a Korean War epic from *Shiri* director Kang Je-gyu featuring stars Jang Dong-gun (*Friend*) and Won Bin. Budgeted at a record 14.7 billion won ($12.8 million), the film utilised vast sets and elaborate pyrotechnics in illustrating the story of two brothers drafted together into the South Korean army. Although not what one might call revisionist history, the film did introduce some new elements into the long tradition of Korean war films, in that it portrayed atrocities by Southern as well as Northern soldiers, and saw one of its heroes switch over to fight for the Northern side towards the end of the film. But the work's primary draw for local audiences was its dramatic (and melodramatic) portrayal of a nation that lived through tremendous upheaval and suffering, ultimately shaping the kind of country that exists today. *Tae Guk Gi*'s plumbing of national sentiment proved capable of drawing not only younger audiences, but also viewers in their sixties and seventies who remembered the war, and were visiting a movie theatre for the first time in decades in a kind of collective remembrance. Released on 6 February, the film sold tickets at an even faster rate than *Silmido*, and ultimately recorded 11.8 million admissions.

The breaking of the ten million admissions barrier ranked as the most dramatic of the many milestones passed by Korean cinema in its decade-long expansion. Newspapers and investigative news programmes gave

	1996	1997	1998	1999	2000	2001	2002	2003	2004	2005	2006	2007
Korean films released	55	60	43	42	62	52	82	65	74	83	108	112
imported films released	320	271	244	233	277	228	192	175	194	215	237	280
total admissions (millions)	42.2	47.5	50.2	54.7	64.6	89.3	105.1	119.5	135.1	145.5	153.4	158.8
market share, domestic films (%)	23.1	25.5	25.1	39.7	35.1	50.1	48.3	53.5	59.3	58.7	63.8	50.80
screens	511	497	507	588	720	818	977	1132	1451	1648	1880	2058
total exports (US $ millions)	0.4m	0.5	3.1	6.0	7.1	11.2	15.0	31.0	58.3	76.0	25.0m	12.3
average budget + p&a (won)	0.9bn + 0.1bn	1.1bn + 0.2bn	1.2bn + 0.3bn	1.4bn + 0.5bn	1.5bn + 0.7bn	1.6bn + 0.9bn	2.5bn + 1.3bn	2.8bn + 1.3bn	2.8bn + 1.4bn	2.7bn + 1.3bn	2.6bn + 1.4bn	2.6bn + 1.2bn
avg. ticket price (won)	4828	5017	5150	5230	5355	5860	6035	6002	6287	6172	6034	6247
exchange rate (won/US$)	850	1016	1333	1175	1139	1275	1214	1194	1151	1028	970	935

Table 2: Film industry statistics, 1996–2007. Source: Korean Cinema Yearbook

the event wide coverage, and also took this opportunity to reassess the growth and current state of the local film industry. Despite the impressive numbers, their conclusions were not always positive. Although audiences showed strong interest in local films, and the industry contained a deep pool of talent, Korea's distribution system was developing in ways that elicited concern. In particular, the accumulation of power by major vertically integrated distributors threatened to make what was already an unlevel playing field even more imbalanced.

In the 1990s, *chaebol* such as Samsung and Daewoo had emulated the classical Hollywood model of a vertically integrated studio with interests in every stage of a film's creation, from investment and production to distribution, exhibition and ancillary markets. However, such companies exited the film industry before they were able to achieve dominance in the exhibition sector, which was the most lucrative and strategically important link in the chain. By the mid-2000s, a new group of distributors had achieved dominance, most notably the film divisions of two giant food conglomerates, the CJ Group (CJ Entertainment) and the Orion Group (Showbox). Both companies were active investors in Korean films – in 2007, CJ Entertainment participated as the main investor on twenty films for a total sum of $86 million. However, the level of their involvement in the exhibition sector gave them an unprecedented degree of power.

As in other territories, the spread of modern multiplexes in Korea was considered to be a strong factor in the increased rate of theatre attendance. The three biggest multiplex chains in order were: CGV, originally structured as a joint venture between Korea's CJ Entertainment, Hong Kong's Golden Village and Australia's Village Roadshow (the latter two would eventually sell their stakes); Lotte Cinema, a division of the massive Korean *chaebol* which focused on building cinemas in its upscale Lotte department stores; and Megabox Cineplex, a joint venture between the Orion Group and US-based Loews Cineplex (which sold its stake in 2006).

Therefore the country's top two distributors controlled two of the most powerful theatre chains. Although both companies took care not to appear to be taking advantage of their situation, in the behind-the-scenes negotiations that form a major part of the distribution process, their weight was clearly felt. Other distributors without their own venues were unable to release films on the same scale, which arguably harmed these films' ability to reach their commercial potential. Over time, the large distributors gained more and more power. In this Korea formed a contrast to the United States, where the Paramount decision of 1948 had forced the Hollywood studios to sell their theatre chains (although under Ronald Reagan's presidency in the 1980s many of them were allowed to start reacquiring venues, in the belief that conglomeration would create stronger, more competitive companies).

Of a nationwide total of 1,100 screens, *Silmido* was released on 325 screens (30%) and *Tae Guk Gi* on a record 430 (39%). Smaller films that had been released at the same time found themselves pushed out of theatres even if they were performing well. The Screen Quota proved to be of no help to small-scale releases, as theatres could simply fulfil their quota obligations by slotting in high grossing Korean blockbusters. How to best support and protect smaller films in the increasingly industrialised Korean film market became an urgent task for policymakers in the coming years.

The Korean Wave

The Korean Wave or *hallyu* can be traced back to 1997–98 when the television drama *What Is Love All About?* (*Sarangi muogillae*) and the boy band H.O.T. began to attract a surprisingly large audience in China and Taiwan (see Shim 2006: 25). From the beginning, it was television serials and pop music rather than cinema that would be *hallyu*'s driving force, but the film industry too would influence (and be influenced by) the phenomenon.

Some of the earliest successes for Korean film came in Hong Kong. Hur Jin-ho's *Christmas in August* (1998) opened on a single screen at the Hong Kong Art Centre in August 1999, but due to unexpectedly strong demand it was shifted to the commercial theatre Broadway Cinematheque in late September. The understated but emotionally stirring melodrama arguably occupied a genre niche that local Hong Kong films had left unfilled, and word-of-mouth was strong. After a lengthy 56-day release, the film's box-office take amounted to HK$795,000 ($100,000) (see Paquet 2007c: 39). Then in November, *Shiri* opened on 15 screens and took the number three slot at the box office in its first week, ultimately grossing HK$6 million ($770,000). Although the film's marketing in Hong Kong focused on actor Han Suk-kyu, the combination of blockbuster-style action and tragic melodrama is also believed to have contributed to its local appeal. A rush of releases would follow: in 2002 alone a total of 22 Korean films were released in the territory, capturing a 4.9% market share. Japan would embrace the new Korean block-buster as well, at least those films with a North Korean theme (given North Korea's close proximity to and hostile attitude towards its former coloniser, such issues were seen as highly relevant to Japan as well). *Shiri* opened in January 2000 and hit number one at the box office, grossing an impressive 1.85 billion yen ($17.6 million), while *JSA* also topped the box office on a massive 235-screen release in May 2001, earning a final tally of 1.2 billion yen ($9.8 million) (see Bak & Nam 2006).

The film that would prove most successful in reaching large audiences in Asia was Kwak Jae-yong's *My Sassy Girl* (*Yeopgijeogin geunyeo*, 2001). Based on a serial novel published on the Internet, the film chronicles the adventures of a university student, Gyeon-woo (singer/actor Cha Tae-hyun) who starts dating a pretty but rather unpredictable and aggressive young woman with a drinking problem (Jun Ji-hyun, who would develop her role in this hit into one of Asia's most prominent modelling careers). The film derives much of its humour from its upending of gender stereotypes, with The Girl (she is never given a name) picking fights in public and shouting threats to her obedient boyfriend. Yet the film clearly lacks any feminist agenda, in that The Girl's domineering attitude is later explained away as a kind of pathological response to personal trauma, and she begins to assume much more traditional gender roles. The film's saccharine conclusion thus beats a retreat into the patriarchal status quo. More of interest is the way the narrative captures a sense of confusion over morals and gender relations in a society upended by furiously accelerated modernisation. With parental figures looming in the background, the protagonist picks his way through a minefield of choices regarding everything from sex to holding hands to emotional commitment. If many iconic comedies succeed by targeting society's deep-seated anxieties, then *My Sassy Girl* may express the uneasy tension that exists between slowly eroding traditional values and the uncertainty of the new.

Produced by Shincine, *My Sassy Girl* sold 4.8 million tickets in Korea and then spent two weeks at number one in Hong Kong, grossing HK$10 million ($1.3 million) – more than any Korean film has earned in that territory before or since. In China, where film imports are highly restricted, the film won over a huge audience on pirated DVD, with an estimated ten million copies sold. Its popularity can be seen in the fact that in a 2006 poll, Chinese Internet users asked to name ten words that remind them of South

Korea cited the film's title, together with 'kimchi' and 'tae kwon do'.

Despite the success of a few individual titles, the Korean Wave's biggest impact on the film industry lay in increasing the regional star power of Korean actors. This process gathered pace in 2004 and 2005 with the runaway success of several Korean television serials. *Winter Sonata* (*Gyeoul yeonga*), a television drama starring Bae Yong-joon and Choi Ji-woo, was first broadcast in Japan by an NHK-operated cable channel in April 2003. A rapturous audience response led to a re-broadcast in December, and then in April 2004 it was shown on NHK's main terrestrial channel. By this time Bae was achieving fame on an unprecedented scale, particularly among middle-aged female viewers. Prime Minister Koizumi Junichiro may only have been stating the obvious when he joked that Bae's popularity had exceeded his own. The following year, traditional costume drama *Jewel in the Palace* (*Daejanggeum*) received close to 50% viewer ratings in Hong Kong, where lead actress Lee Young-ae was named Woman of the Year. The programme would be similarly successful in Taiwan and China.

Growing interest in Korean stars went hand in hand with a broader expansion in film exports. Prior to 1998, annual exports of Korean films generally added up to well under $1 million. However the year 1999 saw the launch of Korea's first international sales companies, including both independent firms like Mirovision and Cineclick Asia as well as specialised divisions within major studios such as CJ Entertainment or Cinema Service. By operating booths at major international markets such as Cannes' Marché du Film or the American Film Market, sales companies began to market Korean films directly to international buyers. Due to such companies' efforts, and the growing marketability of Korean films, annual exports jumped to $6 million in 1999, to $15 million in 2002, and to $58 million in 2004.

It was in Japan, the world's second-largest film market, that the most spectacular rise took place. By the peak of the Korean Wave, deals for films featuring major stars were being struck for $3 million to $4 million each, including Lee Myung-Se's *Duelist* (*Hyeongsa*, 2005) starring Gang Dong-won and action film *Running Wild* (*Yasu*, 2006) starring Kwon Sang-woo. The highest price of all was paid for Hur Jin-ho's *April Snow* (*Oechul*, 2005) starring Bae Yong-joon in his first film role since 2003; although not publicly announced, the deal was rumoured to be at least $7 million. Of the record $76 million in Korean cinema's export earnings in 2005, an astonishing $60 million was made from sales to Japan.

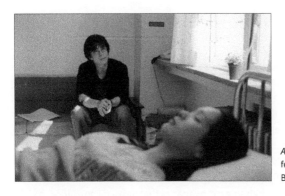

April Snow (2005):
featuring *hallyu* star
Bae Yong-joon

All of these developments were completely new for Korea, and numerous commentators struggled to make sense of what was happening and what it all meant. Cho Hae-Joang (2005) divides the various responses and arguments surrounding the Korean Wave into three broad groups. The first she terms the 'cultural nationalist perspective', which proposed various reasons for the spread of Korean pop culture vis-a-vis American or Japanese cultural products, including Korea's embrace of Confucian family values or the presence of anti-Japanese sentiment in the rest of Asia. The 'neoliberal perspective' focused on the mass-market appeal of Korean pop culture, and the development of new markets and distribution networks in the Asian region. Finally the 'postcolonialist perspective' was taken up primarily by cultural researchers interested in modernisation and global shifts, and considered among other issues the building of an Asian 'cultural bloc'.

The content of Korean films was inevitably affected by *hallyu*. Any film that was being packaged around a major star had to incorporate a narrative that would maintain and build on the actor's pre-existing image. A growing belief that casting, rather than original content or a well-developed screenplay, was the surest route to profitability discouraged a focus on quality. By 2005 and 2006 critics were deriding the trend for quickly-developed, star-centered projects such as *Now and Forever* (*Yeolliji*, 2006), about not one but two protagonists with fatal illnesses, or the Korea-Hong Kong co-production *Daisy* (*Deiji*, 2006) starring Jun Ji-hyun, that were obviously trying to replicate its stars' past successes. Ultimately the majority of such films performed poorly both in Korea and other Asian markets, setting the stage for the later waning of the Korean Wave.

The Host

Bong Joon-ho's *The Host* opens in a mortuary at the 8th US Army base in central Seoul. An American officer, fretting over several hundred dusty bottles of formaldehyde, orders a Korean private to empty them into the sink. The private tries to object, noting that the drain leads into the Han River, but he is overruled and soon the carcinogenic substance is trickling towards Seoul's famous waterway. Several years later, something begins to stir in the Han River: a truck-sized amphibian mutant that has developed a taste for human flesh.

The Host, a genre-bending extravaganza that broke all box-office records on its release in July 2006, is a film with a keen and ironic sense of history. The scene at the mortuary is based on a real-life incident which sparked an uproar on its exposure by an environmental watch group in 2000. Although the director's utilisation of this episode as a kind of creation myth is play-fully tongue-in-cheek, its presence here also functions as a reminder of how events from the past can return to impact the present in unpredictable ways. Later scenes in the film, in which the creature visits destruction upon the people of Seoul, are meant to evoke memories of previous disasters that would be familiar to its audience: the collapse of Seongsu Bridge in 1994, the crushing of two schoolgirls by a US tank in 2002, the Daegu subway fire in 2003, not to mention SARS and the Iraq War.

Meanwhile the film's protagonists, a family that runs a food stand next to the Han River, are also linked to recent Korean history. Their means of employment betray their past, in that the right to operate the Han River food stands were the sole compensation provided to residents of the Sanggye-dong slum, after their neighbourhood was levelled in a 'beau-tification campaign' before the 1988 Olympics (as depicted in Kim Dong-won's documentary *Sanggye-dong Olympics*). Each character may also be seen as representing a different decade of Korean history: Hee-bong (Byun Hee-bong), the 1960s patriarch who struggled to raise his family amidst poverty; Gang-du (Song Kang-ho), who appears mentally affected by the traumas of the 1970s; Nam-il (Park Hae-il), a Molotov-cocktail throwing veteran of the 1980s student movement, currently drunk and unemployed; Nam-joo (Bae Doo-na), an amateur competitive archer of the subsequent generation who seems unable to realise her significant potential; and the

Bong Joon-ho's *The Host* (2006) sold over 13 million tickets

industrious and levelheaded Hyun-seo (Ko A-sung), a middle school student representing the 2000s who is captured by the monster at the start of the film.

The Host's central conflict is the family's struggle to save Hyun-seo from the monster's grasp. The family is nothing if not dysfunctional, but the initiative and passion they display in their search forms a strong contrast to the misguided and incompetent efforts of the Korean and US governments to contain the situation. Ultimately, the four bereaved family members spend more time fighting health professionals, military personnel and representatives of the government than the monster itself.

Ultimately selling just over 13 million tickets in its home country (equivalent to 27% of the populace), *The Host* was a landmark work in any number of respects. Mixing a creative approach to genre with sociopolitical commentary and big-budget spectacle, the film doubles as both a blockbuster and a work of auteur cinema. With creature modelling carried out at New Zealand's Weta Studios, computer-generated effects supplied by San Francisco-based The Orphanage, and the film's first confirmed financing coming from Japan (Happinet Corp.) instead of Korea, the making of the film involved talent and resources from around the world. Pre-release hype grew strong after its premiere at the Cannes Film Festival's Directors Fortnight section, and reached fever pitch before its summer release, when marketing/distribution giant Showbox (a division of the Orion group) opened the film with a record 620 prints – over a third of the nation's screens. Budgeted at $11 million, it earned the equivalent of $17.2 million on its first weekend, and $97 million by the end of its theatrical run (see Paquet 2007b). International sales agent Cineclick Asia sold a total $5.9 million in foreign distribution deals, though it would perform better in some territories (China, the US, Spain, Singapore) than in others (Japan, the UK, Hong Kong).

The Host represents the final maturation of Korean cinema in terms of its growth from a weak, highly regulated industry that operated under the government's hand to a competitive, globalised business that could turn out almost any kind of film. The end result of that maturation produced ambivalent feelings in many observers, who worried that commercial forces were starting to overpower the filmmaking process. And yet Bong, whose right to final cut on *The Host* was never challenged, had created a work of surprising originality and depth. It seems appropriate that this film, with its contradictory mix of commercial power, artistic precision and sociopolitical commentary, should represent the high water mark of Korean cinema's post-democratic boom.

Independent films in the twenty-first century

The independent film movement had functioned as a close-knit community in the 1990s, turning out short films, documentaries and the occasional feature-length work that strove to highlight its independence from capital interests and the mainstream film industry. During the industrialisation and commercial success of Korean films in the following decade, independent films did not fade but rather underwent a significant expansion. Although the increased diversity of subject matter and shooting styles led to an occasional blurring of the lines between mainstream and independent aesthetics, the overall health of the independent film sector in the latter part of the decade served as a point of optimism as the fortunes of the mainstream industry began to slide.

As in other countries, one of the most significant shifts to take place over this period was the decreased cost of making feature films due to new digital technologies. Whereas short films had formerly occupied the central position in Korean independent film, by the mid-2000s many aspiring filmmakers were choosing to finance their own feature debuts (often at great personal sacrifice). By 2008 it was even becoming common for students and film programmes to shoot feature-length films as their graduation projects.

Leading figures in the independent film movement had also turned their efforts to expanding distribution opportunities for features and documentaries. Taking advantage of financial and logistical support from the Korean Film Council, filmmakers were successful in securing theatrical releases for large numbers of independent films. Whereas only four films released in 2004 had a budget of less than 1 billion won ($900,000), by 2008 this number had expanded to 38 or 35% of the total.

One notable example of a film that took full advantage of its independent status to pursue an aggressively non-mainstream vision is Kim Gok and Kim Sun's *Capitalist Manifesto: Working Men of All Countries, Accumulate!* (*Jabondang seoneon: mangukui nodongjayeo, chukjeokhara!*, 2003). Playfully channeling Karl Marx to illustrate the instabilities and pitfalls of the capitalist system, the Kim brothers structure their film as a system of repetitive transactions between dull-eyed protagonists who act like cogs in a machine. In place of a conventional narrative, scenes involving prostitutes and gangsters are presented and re-presented with various elements changed until the entire system lurches towards crisis.

Other films stood out for their foregrounding of non-mainstream perspectives. Leesong Hee-il, the most prominent of Korea's openly gay filmmakers, first made a name for himself with highly praised short films such as *Sugar Hill* (2000) and *Good Romance* (2001). His feature debut *No Regret* (*Huhoehaji anha*, 2006) details the relationship between a prostitute in a gay bar and a man from a rich, conservative family who refuse to acknowledge his sexual orientation. After premiering at the Pusan International Film Festival, the low-budget film enjoyed a surprisingly successful commercial release, earning a higher rate of return than even *The Host*.

Meanwhile the career of Zhang Lu illustrates the increasingly transnational character of Korean cinema. An ethnic Korean from Yanbian, China, Zhang worked as a novelist before making his debut as a filmmaker with the assistance of Korean producer Choi Doo-young. Insisting on the universal, transnational nature of his work, Zhang locates many of his films in vaguely defined spaces in which various ethnicities interact. *Grain in Ear* (*Mangjong*, 2005) focuses on an ethnic Korean widow who sells *kimchi* in an undefined Chinese town. *Desert Dream* (*Gyeonggye*, 2007) is set in Mongolia at the edge of the Gobi Desert, and presents an encounter between a Mongolian man and a North Korean refugee who arrives with her son. Although still a Chinese citizen, Zhang has received various kinds of financial support from the Korean Film Council and has been embraced wholeheartedly by the Korean film community. He has also taken advantage of his position to support other ethnic Korean filmmakers in China, producing works such as Jin Guang-hao's *Life Track* (*Guedo*, 2007) which won the top award at the 2007 Pusan International Film Festival.

The bubble bursts

Analysing industry statistics for the year 2006 reveals a contradiction. In one sense, it was the most successful year ever for Korean cinema. Not only *The Host*, but period drama *King and the Clown* (*Wangui namja*) by director Lee Joon-ik also emerged as an unexpected smash hit, selling 12.3 million tickets. Both the market share of Korean cinema (63.8%) and overall theatrical admissions (153.4 million tickets) reached astounding levels compared to the lows of a decade earlier. One might think that the Korean film industry would have been celebrating its successes, but the mood was sombre. In fact, apart from the producers of a few runaway hit films, almost everyone in the film industry was losing money. Part of the problem was that the number of mainstream commercial films being produced had risen to unsustainable levels. During the production boom of 2005 and 2006, so many films were being shot that producers faced a shortage of cameras, and began to talk of borrowing equipment from Japan or China. By the time this glut of films reached theatres, cutthroat competition made it difficult for any of them to turn a profit.

More seriously, the basic economics of feature film production in Korea were being called into question. Throughout the boom period, the cost of making films had steadily grown, affected by star salaries, labour costs and rising technical standards. When exports to Japan were booming, producers could afford to absorb these extra costs. However, as interest in the Korean Wave began to wane, overall exports crashed from $76 million in 2005 to $24.5 million in 2006 and only $12.3 million in 2007. Without the prospect of earning a six- or seven-figure guarantee from a sale to Japan, Korean films had to depend almost exclusively on their (highly unpredictable) performance in domestic theatres.

The Korean film industry's most serious commercial vulnerability vis-a-vis Hollywood was the lack of a healthy market for DVDs and other ancillary products. Whereas US films received a majority of their revenues from

DVD, cable television, merchandising and other sources, the situation in the Korean film industry resembled Hollywood in the 1970s, when theatrical admissions accounted for 70–80% of overall revenues. For example, in 2006 DVD sales in Korea (excluding rentals) were the equivalent of $72 million, compared to theatrical revenues of $954 million. By contrast, in the same year the US market for DVD sales was $16.6 billion compared to $9.49 billion in theatrical revenues (Anon. 2007). The most commonly cited reason for the weakness of DVD in Korea was online piracy, which gained an early foothold in South Korea thanks to the country's edge in broadband Internet technologies.

The end result of this was that films that failed at the box office had little or no second chance to recover profits on DVD. Given that distribution patterns had moved towards the Hollywood model of the wide release, with just a handful of films saturating the nation's screens during peak seasons, smaller films that depended on word of mouth were particularly disadvantaged.

The industry's basic structural problems together with the burst bubble in film finance led to a deep slump in 2007 and 2008. Venture capital investors, after suffering heavy losses, reduced their investment in Korean films or pulled out entirely. Producers began looking for ways to lower costs, from shooting on digital cameras to choosing less technically demanding projects. The geographical centre of the film industry, which had coalesced in the business/financial district of Gangnam in Seoul, began to disperse as film companies sought neighbourhoods with cheaper rent. Fewer and fewer mainstream commercial projects were being produced (although the number of low-budget independent features continued to rise). Worries began to spread that, unable to find work, experienced technicians and crew members were leaving the film industry. Meanwhile a collapse in the stock prices of many entertainment firms, which had achieved 'backdoor' listings on the local stock exchange during the boom years, caused additional turmoil (see Paquet 2009).

Compounding the gloom was the fact that in early 2006 the Korean government had bowed to long-standing pressure from the US and reduced Korea's Screen Quota to 73 days per year, from its previous level of 106–46. The move was made as a prelude to talks on a US-South Korea Free Trade Agreement. Filmmakers felt betrayed, and nearly a year of large and small demonstrations, both in Korea and at international film festivals, ensued. Most memorable were a long series of single-person protests held by directors, actors, producers and other members of the film industry in various locations throughout Seoul. By this time, the public's support of the quota system had waned compared to in 1998, when the industry was much weaker. Although the quota's practical effect on the film industry was uncertain in a time when market shares remained above 40% and most theatres were owned by local distributors, its reduction was a psychological and political blow, and distracted the film industry from addressing other of its structural problems.

After the box-office peak of 2006, Korean audiences started becoming noticeably more selective about their consumption of domestic films. Market share fell to 51% in 2007 and 43% in 2008. Whereas in the middle of the decade, politicians boasted about the strength of Korean film and spoke of using cinema as a kind of 'soft power' to improve the nation's standing within Asia, a few years later all talk had turned to addressing the industry's weaknesses. Nonetheless there remained deep pools of talent within the Korean filmmaking community, and the more notable work produced each year continued to screen at major festivals and open in foreign markets. The end of Korea's boom and bubble was more of a humbling than a crash.

5   CONCLUSION

The late twentieth century saw all manner of 'new waves' and 'new cinemas' from around the world capture the attention of critics and scholars. Film movements are generally defined as an injection of creative energy and new talent into a filmmaking community, resulting for a given time in a new kind of film. David Bordwell and Kristin Thompson define film movements with two statements: '(1) films that are produced within a particular period and/or nation and that share significant traits of style and form; and (2) filmmakers who operate within a common production structure and who share certain assumptions about filmmaking' (1997: 441).

Certainly New Korean Cinema conforms in a broad sense to the latter statement, given filmmakers' collective efforts to modernise the film industry, and their consensus on the need to distance themselves from the Korean films of their recent past. Regarding the former statement, although it is not primarily an aesthetic or thematic-based movement such as Italian Neorealism, young Korean directors' prioritising of imagery, their targeting of young audiences and their experimentation with genre also provide for a degree of stylistic continuity within the overall diversity of the movement.

Nonetheless, New Korean Cinema was a phenomenon that differed from most other film movements. What happened between the late 1980s and the mid-2000s was more than just the arrival of a new generation of directors or the flowering of a new cinematic style. Throughout much of the twentieth century, the Korean film industry had been pinned into an unnatural position by regulations and restrictions that hampered its growth and prevented a normal course of development. When change finally came, it manifested itself not as a brilliant offshoot of an otherwise stable system, but as a broad-based slide towards a new equilibrium. The Korean film community had moved beyond its authoritarian past and finally succeeded in creating a 'normal' film industry.

After a decade of rapid change, by the mid- to late-2000s many people in the Korean film industry began to sense that a new era was beginning. It was not that the aesthetics of Korean cinema had moved in a new direction, or that the major figures of the movement had experienced a change in fortune. By the mid-2000s, the directors most commonly associated with New Korean Cinema, such as Park Chan-wook, Bong Joon-ho, Lee Chang-dong and others, were still at the start of what may turn out to be long and fruitful careers. Large numbers of new directors continued to make their debut each year. In this sense, the movement was still very much alive.

However, the burst of energy that had been released by broader social changes and structural reforms to the industry had begun to dissipate. The year 2006 can be seen as a meaningful endpoint for several important aspects of New Korean Cinema. That dramatic year, which saw two films (*King and the Clown* and *The Host*) set box-office records, was seen even at the time as a likely high water mark for the commercial industry. At the same time, the bursting of the film finance bubble and the retreat of the Korean Wave caused widespread anxiety among producers and filmmakers.

What had run its course by 2007 and 2008 was the feverish rate of change that had done so much to transform Korean cinema over the previous two decades. Much of that change – from regulatory reforms to new industrial practices to the turbulent social shifts that accompanied Korea's democratisation – had created an environment in which new visions and new voices were given an unusual freedom to experiment. Not only that, but the more successful of those voices were quickly able to take up positions of leadership in the evolving industry.

The more mature industry that emerged at the end of those years was also in many ways supportive of creative talent. Film directors continued to retain a significant degree of creative control compared to their counterparts in other countries including the US. The continually evolving technological capabilities of the industry gave filmmakers a wide range of choices in realising their creative vision. South Korean society remained, on the whole, highly supportive of domestic cinema in terms of audience interest, prominent coverage in the media and the level of investment received from government and industry.

However, the era that had passed was unique in Korean film history, standing out for its combination of new talent, risk taking, rapid change and quickly rising ambitions. An entirely new filmmaking community had emerged in those years, and refashioned public perceptions of local cinema. Korean film had also moved from the fringes of world cinema to become an influential contributor to Asian cultural currents and a mainstay on the international festival circuit. Not so much a renewal, the process might better be described as a rebirth. Korean cinema had entered the twenty-first century with a new identity.

FILMOGRAPHY

batteries not included (Matthew Robbins, 1987, US)

2009 Lost Memories (*2009 roseuteu memorijeu*) (Lee Si-myung, 2002, S Korea)

301,302 (*Samgongil samgongi*) (Park Chul-soo, 1995, S Korea)

3-Iron (*Bin jip*) (Kim Ki-duk, 2004, S Korea)

3PM Bathhouse Paradise (*Eoksutang*) (Kwak Kyung-taek, 1996, S Korea)

A Bittersweet Life (*Dalkomhan insaeng*) (Kim Jee-woon, 2005, S Korea)

A Good Lawyer's Wife (*Baramnan gajok*) (Im Sang-soo, 2003, S Korea)

A Hot Roof (*Gaegateun narui ohu*) (Lee Min-yong, 1995, S Korea)

A Petal (*Kkonnip*) (Jang Sun-woo, 1996, S Korea)

A Single Spark (*Areumdaun cheongnyeon jeontaeil*) (Park Kwang-su, 1995, S Korea)

A Small Ball Shot by a Dwarf (*Nanjangiga ssoaollin jageungong*) (Lee Won-se, 1981, S Korea)

A Tale of Two Sisters (*Janghwa, hongnyeon*) (Kim Jee-woon, 2003, S Korea)

Adada (*Adada*) (Im Kwon-taek, 1988, S Korea)

Adventures of Mrs. Park, The (*Bakbonggon gachulsageon*) (Kim Tae-kyun, 1996, S Korea)

Age of Success (*Seonggongsidae*) (Jang Sun-woo, 1988, S Korea)

An Affair (*Jeongsa*) (E J-yong, 1998, S Korea)

April Snow (*Oechul*) (Hur Jin-ho, 2005, S Korea)

Art Museum by the Zoo (*Misulgwanyeop dongmurwon*) (Lee Jeong-hyang, 1998, S Korea)

Asako in Ruby Shoes (*Sunaebo*) (E J-yong, 2000, S Korea-Japan)

Attack the Gas Station! (*Juyuso seupgyeok sageon*) (Kim Sang-jin, 1999, S Korea)

Baby Sale (*Beibi seil*) (Kim Bonn, 1997, S Korea)

Bad Guy (*Nappeun namja*) (Kim Ki-duk, 2002, S Korea)

Bad Movie (*Nappeun yeonghwa*) (Jang Sun-woo, 1997, S Korea)
Berlin Report (*Bereullin ripoteu*) (Park Kwang-su, 1991, S Korea)
Bet on My Disco (*Haejeok diseuko wang doeda*) (Kim Dong-won, 2002, S
    Korea)
Between the Knees (*Mureupgwa mureup sai*) (Lee Jang-ho, 1984, S Korea)
Birdcage Inn (*Parandaemun*) (Kim Ki-duk, 1998, S Korea)
Black Republic (*Geudeuldo uricheoreom*) (Park Kwang-su, 1990, S Korea)
Blue in You, The (*Geudaeanui beullu*) (Lee Hyeon-seung, 1992, S Korea)
Bravo My Life (*Saranghae malsunssi*) (Park Heung-sik, 2005, S Korea)
Cable Guy, The (Ben Stiller, 1996, US)
Capitalist Manifesto: Working Men of All Countries, Accumulate!
    (*Jabondang seoneon: mangukui nodongjayeo, chukjeokhara!*) (Kim
    Gok and Kim Sun, 2003, S Korea)
Chaser, The (*Chugyeokjja*) (Na Hong-jin, 2008, S Korea)
Children of Darkness (*Eodumui jasikdeul*) (Lee Jang-ho, 1981, S Korea)
Chilsu and Mansu (*Chilsuwa mansu*) (Park Kwang-su, 1988, S Korea)
Christmas in August (*Palworui keuriseumaseu*) (Hur Jin-ho, 1998, S Korea)
Come Come Come Upward (*Ajeaje baraaje*) (Im Kwon-taek, 1989, S Korea)
Conduct Zero (*Pumhaengjero*) (Joh Keun-shik, 2002, S Korea)
Contact, The (*Jeopsok*) (Chang Youn-hyun, 1997, S Korea)
Crocodile (*Ageo*) (Kim Ki-duk, 1996, S Korea)
Daisy (*Deiji*) (Andrew Lau, 2006, Hong Kong/S Korea)
Day a Pig Fell into the Well, The (*Dwaejiga umure ppajin nal*) (Hong
    Sangsoo, 1996, S Korea)
Declaration of Fools (*Baboseoneon*) (Lee Jang-ho, 1983, S Korea)
Deep Blue Night (*Gipgo pureun bam*) (Bae Chang-ho, 1985, S Korea)
Delicatessen (Marc Caro and Jean-Pierre Jeunet, 1991, France)
Desert Dream (*Gyeonggye* aka *Hyazgar*) (Zhang Lu, 2007, S Korea/France)
Ditto (*Donggam*) (Kim Jung-kwon, 2000, S Korea)
Dr. K (*Dakteokei*) (Kwak Kyung-taek, 1999, S Korea)
Duelist (*Hyeongsa*) (Lee Myung-Se, 2005, S Korea)
Emmanuelle (Just Jaeckin, 1974, France)
Eo-u-dong (*Eoudong*) (Lee Jang-ho, 1985, S Korea)
E.T.: The Extra-Terrestrial (Steven Spielberg, 1982, US)
Fallen Angels (*Duo luo tian shi*) (Wong Kar Wai, 1995, Hong Kong)
Farewell My Darling (*Haksaengbugunsinwi*) (Park Chul-soo, 1996, S
    Korea)

Fatal Attraction (Adrian Lyne, 1987, US)

Festival (*Chukje*) (Im Kwon-taek, 1996, S Korea)

Fine Windy Day (*Baram bureo joeun nal*) (Lee Jang-ho, 1980, S Korea)

Firebird (*Bulse*) (Kim Young-bin, 1997, S Korea)

First Love (*Cheotsarang*) (Lee Myung-Se, 1993, S Korea)

Five Fingers of Death (*Tian xia di yi quan*) (Chung Chang-hwa, 1972, Hong Kong)

Foul King, The (*Banchikwang*) (Kim Jee-woon, 2000, S Korea)

Fox with Nine Tails, The (*Gumiho*) (Park Heon-soo, 1994, S Korea)

Friend (*Chingu*) (Kwak Kyung-taek, 2001, S Korea)

Gagman (*Gaegeumaen*) (Lee Myung-Se, 1989, S Korea)

Gate of Destiny, The (*Gwicheondo*) (Lee Gyeong-young, 1996, S Korea)

Genealogy, The (*Jokbo*) (Im Kwon-taek, 1978, S Korea)

General's Son, The (*Janggunui adeul*) (Im Kwon-taek, 1990, S Korea)

Ghost Mama (*Goseuteu mama*) (Han Ji-seung, 1996, S Korea)

Gilsottum (*Gilsotteum*) (Im Kwon-taek, 1985, S Korea)

Gingko Bed, The (*Eunhaengnamuchimdae*) (Kang Je-kyu, 1996, S Korea)

Good, the Bad, the Weird, The (*Joeunnom nappeunnom isanghannom*) (Kim Jee-woon, 2008, S Korea)

Grain in Ear (*Mangjong*) (Zhang Lu, 2005, China/S Korea)

Green Fish (*Chorogmulgogi*) (Lee Chang-dong, 1997, S Korea)

Habitual Sadness (*Najeun moksori 2*) (Byun Young-joo, 1997, S Korea)

Happiness Does Not Depend on School Records (*Haengbogeun seongjeok suni anijanayo*) (Kang Woo-suk, 1989, S Korea)

Happy End (*Haepi endeu*) (Jung Ji-woo, 1999, S Korea)

Happy Together (*Chun gwong cha sit*) (Wong Kar Wai, 1997, Hong Kong)

Heat (Michael Mann, 1995, US)

Hi Dharma (*Dalmaya nolja*) (Park Cheol-kwan, 2001, S Korea)

Hidden Hero, The (*Gitbareomneun gisu*) (Im Kwon-taek, 1979, S Korea)

Hometown of the Stars (*Byeoldeurui gohyang*) (Lee Jang-ho, 1974, S Korea)

Host, The (*Goemul*) (Bong Joon-ho, 2006, S Korea)

Housemaid, The (*Hanyeo*) (Kim Ki-young, 1960, S Korea)

How to Top My Wife (*Manura jugigi*) (Kang Woo-suk, 1994, S Korea)

Hwa-Om-Kyung (*Hwaeomgyeong*) (Jang Sun-woo, 1993, S Korea)

Inch'Allah (*Insyalla*) (Lee Min-yong, 1996, S Korea)

Indiana Jones and the Last Crusade (Steven Spielberg, 1989, US)

Indochina (*Indochine*) (Régis Wargnier, 1992, France)

Insect Woman (Chungnyeo) (Kim Ki-young, 1972, S Korea)
Iodo (Ieodo) (Kim Ki-young, 1977, S Korea)
Isle, The (Seom) (Kim Ki-duk, 2000, S Korea)
Ivan the Mercenary (Yongbyeong-iban) (Lee Hyeon-seok, 1997, S Korea)
Joint Security Area (Gongdonggyeongbiguyeok JSA) (Park Chan-wook,
     2000, S Korea)
Jungle Story, (Jeonggeul seutori) (Kim Hong-joon, 1996, S Korea)
Jurassic Park (Steven Spielberg, 1993, US)
Kick the Moon (Sillaui dalbam) (Kim Sang-jin, 2001, S Korea)
King and the Clown (Wangui namja) (Lee Joon-ik, 2006, S Korea)
Kuro Arirang (Guro arirang) (Park Chong-won, 1989, S Korea)
Lady Vengeance (Chinjeolhan geumjassi) (Park Chan-wook, 2005, S Korea)
Last Empress, The (Mo dai huang hou) (Chen Jialin and Li Han Hsiang,
     1986, China)
Last Witness, The (Choehuui jeungin) (Lee Doo-yong, 1980, S Korea)
Letter, The (Pyeonji) (Lee Jeong-guk, 1997, S Korea)
Libera Me (Ribera me) (Yang Yun-ho, 2000, S Korea)
Lies (Geojinmal) (Jang Sun-woo, 1999, S Korea)
Life Track (Guedo) (Jin Guang-hao, 2007, China-S Korea)
Living Daylights, The (John Glen, 1987, UK/US)
Lover, The (L'amant) (Jean-Jacques Annaud, 1992, France/UK/Vietnam)
Lovers of Woomook-baemi, The (Umukbaemiui sarang) (Jang Sun-woo,
     1990, S Korea)
Lovers on the Bridge, The (Les amants du Pont-Neuf) (Leos Carax, 1991,
     France)
Madame Aema (Aemabuin) (Jeong In-yeop, 1982, S Korea)
Man With Three Coffins, The (Nageuneneun gireseodo swiji anneunda)
     (Lee Jang-ho, 1987, S Korea)
Mandala (Mandara) (Im Kwon-taek, 1981, S Korea)
Manon of the Spring (Manon des sources) (Claude Berri, 1986, Italy/
     France)
March of Fools (Babodeurui haengjin) (Ha Kil-jong, 1975, S Korea)
Marriage Story (Gyeolhoniyagi) (Kim Ui-seok, 1992, S Korea)
Marrying the Mafia (Gamunui yeonggwang) (Chung Hung-soon, 2002, S
     Korea)
May 18 (Hwaryeohan hyuga) (Kim Ji-hoon, 2007, S Korea)
Memories of Murder (Sarinui chueok) (Bong Joon-ho, 2003, S Korea)

Mister Mama (*Miseuteo mama*) (Kang Woo-suk, 1992, S Korea)

Mom's Got a Lover (*Eommaege aeini saenggyeosseoyo*) (Kim Dong-bin, 1995, S Korea)

Moscow Does Not Believe in Tears (*Moskva slezam ne verit*) (Vladimir Menshov, 1980, Soviet Union)

Mother (*Eomi*) (Park Chul-soo, 1985, S Korea)

Mr. Gam's Victory (*Syupeoseuta gamsayong*) (Kim Jong-hyun, 2004, S Korea)

Mulberry Tree (*Ppong*) (Lee Doo-yong, 1985, S Korea)

Mulleya, Mulleya (*Mulleya, mulleya*) (Lee Doo-yong, 1984, S Korea)

Murmuring, The (*Najeun moksori*) (Byun Young-joo, 1995, S Korea)

My Boss, My Hero (*Dusabuilche*) (Youn JK., 2001, S Korea)

My Korean Cinema (*Naui hangugyeonghwa*) (Kim Hong-joon, 2003, S Korea)

My Love My Bride (*Naui sarang naui sinbu*) (Lee Myung-Se, 1990, S Korea)

My Nike (*Mutjima paemilli*) (Park Kwang-hyun, 2002, S Korea)

My Own Breathing (*Sumgyeol*) (Byun Young-joo, 1999, S Korea)

My Sassy Girl (*Yeopgijeogin geunyeo*) (Kwak Jae-yong, 2001, S Korea)

My Wife Is a Gangster (*Jopong manura*) (Jo Jin-kyu, 2001, S Korea)

Natural City (*Naechyureol siti*) (Min Byung-chun, 2003, S Korea)

Night and Day (*Bamgwa nat*) (Hong Sangsoo, 2007, S Korea)

Night Before the Strike (*Paeopjeonya*) (Lee Eun-gi, Lee Jae-gu, Chang Youn-hyun, Chang Dong-hong, 1990, S Korea)

Night Voyage (*Yahaeng*) (Kim Soo-yong, 1977, S Korea)

No Regret (*Huhoehaji anha*) (Leesong Hee-il, 2006, S Korea)

No. 3 (*Neombeo 3*) (Song Neung-han, 1997, S Korea)

Now and Forever (*Yeolliji*) (Kim Seong-jung, 2006, S Korea)

Nowhere to Hide (*Injeongsajeongbolgeot eopta*) (Lee Myung-Se, 1999, S Korea)

Oasis (*Oasiseu*) (Lee Chang-dong, 2002, S Korea)

Oh! Land of Dreams (*O! kkumui nara*) (Lee Eun-gi, Chang Youn-hyun, Chang Dong-hong, 1988, S Korea)

Oldboy (*Oldeuboi*) (Park Chan-wook, 2003, S Korea)

Once Upon a Time in America (Sergio Leone, 1984, Italy/US)

Only Because You Are a Woman (*Danji geudaega yeojaraneun iyumaneuro*) (Kim Yoo-jin, 1991, S Korea)

Opening the Closed School Gate (*Dachin gyomuneul yeolmyeo*) (Lee Jae-gu, Choi Ho, Kim Suk, Kim Geon, Kang Kyeong-hwan, Hwang Gil-jae, 1991, S Korea)

Our Twisted Hero (*Urideurui ilgeureojin yeongung*) (Park Chong-won, 1992, S Korea)

Pannori Arirang (*Pannori Arirang*) (Park Kwang-su, Kim Hong-joon, Hwang Qu-dok, Moon Won-lip, 1983, S Korea)

Partisans of South Korea (*Nambugun*) (Chung Ji-young, 1990, S Korea)

Peemak (*Pimak*) (Lee Doo-yong, 1980, S Korea)

People in a Slum (*Kkobangdongnesaramdeul*) (Bae Chang-ho, 1982, S Korea)

People in White, The (*Geomeuna ttange hina baekseong*) (Bae Yong-kyoon, 1996, S Korea)

Peppermint Candy (*Bakasatang*) (Lee Chang-dong, 1999, S Korea)

Piagol (*Piagol*) (Lee Kang-cheon, 1955, S Korea)

Pillar of Mist (*Angaegidung*) (Park Chul-soo, 1986, S Korea)

Power of Kangwon Province, The (*Gangwondoui him*) (Hong Sangsoo, 1998, S Korea)

President's Last Bang, The (*Geuttae geusaramdeul*) (Im Sang-soo, 2004, S Korea)

Project A (*'A' gai wak*) (Jackie Chan, 1983, Hong Kong)

Public Enemy (*Gonggongui jeok*) (Kang Woo-suk, 2002, S Korea)

Quiet Family, The (*Joyonghan gajok*) (Kim Jee-woon, 1998, S Korea)

R U Ready? (*A yu redi?*) (Yoon Sang-ho, 2002, S Korea)

Rain Man (Barry Levinson, 1988, US)

Red Hunt (*Redeu heonteu*) (Cho Seong-bong, 1996, S Korea)

Resurrection of the Little Match Girl (*Seongnyangpari sonyeoui jaerim*) (Jang Sun-woo, 2002, S Korea)

Road Taken, The (*Seontaek*) (Hong Ki-seon, 2003, S Korea)

Road to Sampo (*Sampo ganeun gil*) (Lee Man-hee, 1975, S Korea)

Road to the Racetrack (*Gyeongmajang ganeungil*) (Jang Sun-woo, 1991, S Korea)

R-Point (*Alpointeu*) (Kong Su-chang, 2004, S Korea)

Rub Love (*Reobeureobeu*) (Lee Seo-gun, 1997, S Korea)

Running Wild (*Yasu*) (Kim Sung-soo, 2006, S Korea)

Sacrifice, The (*Offret*) (Andrei Tarkovsky, 1986, Sweden/UK/France)

Salesman (Albert Maysles and David Maysles, 1968, US)

Samaritan Girl (*Samaria*) (Kim Ki-duk, 2004, S Korea)

Sanggye-dong Olympics (*Sanggyedong ollimpik*) (Kim Dong-won, 1987, S Korea)

Save the Green Planet (*Jigureul jikyeora*) (Jang Joon-hwan, 2003, S Korea)

Secret Sunshine (*Miryang*) (Lee Chang-dong, 2007, S Korea)

Seven Days in Tibet (Jean-Jacques Annaud, 1997, US)

Seven Women Prisoners (*7inui yeoporo*) (Lee Man-hee, 1965, S Korea)

Sex Is Zero (*Saekjeuksigong*) (Youn JK., 2002 S Korea)

Shiri (*Swiri*) (Kang Je-kyu, 1998, S Korea)

Silent Assassins (Lee Doo-yong, Scott Thomas, 1988, US)

Silmido (*Silmido*) (Kang Woo-suk, 2003, S Korea)

Silver Stallion (*Eunmaneun oji anneunda*) (Jang Gil-su, 1991, S Korea)

Song of Resurrection (*Buhwarui norae*) (Lee Jeong-guk, 1990, S Korea)

Sopyonje (*Seopyeonje*) (Im Kwon-taek, 1993, S Korea)

Soul Guardians, The (*Toemarok*) (Park K. C., 1998, S Korea)

Spring in My Hometown (*Areumdaun sijeol*) (Lee Kwang-mo, 1998, S Korea)

Spring, Summer, Fall, Winter... and Spring (*Bom yeoreum gaeul gyeoul geurigo bom*) (Kim Ki-duk, 2003, S Korea)

Spy, The (*Gancheop richeoljin*) (Jang Jin, 1999, S Korea)

Suri-se (*Seoul Film Collective*, 1984, S Korea)

Surrogate Mother (*Ssibaji*) (Im Kwon-taek, 1987, S Korea)

Susan Brink's Arirang (*Sujan beuringkeuui arirang*) (Jang Gil-su, 1991, S Korea/Sweden)

Sympathy for Mr. Vengeance (*Boksuneun naui geot*) (Park Chan-wook, 2002, S Korea)

Tae Guk Gi (*Taegeukkki hwinallimyeo*) (Kang Je-kyu, 2004, S Korea)

Taebaek Mountains, The (*Taebaeksanmaek*) (Im Kwon-taek, 1994, S Korea)

Take Care of My Cat (*Goyangireul butakae*) (Jeong Jae-eun, 2001, S Korea)

Take the Money and Run (*Doneul gatgo twieora*) (Kim Sang-jin, 1995, S Korea)

Tazza: The High Rollers (*Tajja*) (Choi Dong-hoon, 2006, S Korea)

Tell Me Something (*Telmisseomding*) (Chang Youn-hyun, 1999, S Korea)

Terminator (James Cameron, 1984, UK/US)

That Man, That Woman (*Geu yeoja, geu namja*) (Kim Ui-seok, 1993, S Korea)

That Summer (*Geu yeoreum*) (Kim Dong-bin, 1984, S Korea)

Their Last Love Affair (*Jidokan saran*) (Lee Myung-Se, 1996, S Korea)

They Shot the Sun (*Geudeureun taeyangeul ssoattta*) (Lee Jang-ho, 1981, S Korea)

Thirst (*Bakjwi*) (Park Chan-wook, 2009, S Korea)

Three Friends (*Se chingu*) (Yim Soon-rye, 1996, S Korea)

Three Ninjas Kick Back (Charles T. Kanganis, 1994, US/Japan)

Time (*Sigan*) (Kim Ki-duk, 2006, S Korea)

To the Starry Island (*Geuseome gagosiptta*) (Park Kwang-su, 1994, S Korea)

To You, From Me (*Neoege nareul bonaenda*) (Jang Sun-woo, 1994, S Korea)

Touch of Evil (Orson Welles, 1958, US)

Tube (*Tyubeu*) (Baek Woon-hak, 2003, S Korea)

Turning Gate (*Saenghwarui balkkyeon*) (Hong Sangsoo, 2002, S Korea)

Two Cops (*Tukapsseu*) (Kang Woo-suk, 1993, S Korea)

Untold Scandal (*Seukaendeul*) (E J-yong, 2003, S Korea)

Virgin Stripped Bare by Her Bachelors (*O! sujeong*) (Hong Sangsoo, 2000, S Korea)

War and Peace (*Voyna i mir*) (Sergei Bondarchuk, 1967, Soviet Union)

Whale Hunting (*Goraesanyang*) (Bae Chang-ho, 1984, S Korea)

What Are You Going to Do Tomorrow (*Naeileun mwohalgeoni*) (Yi Bong-won, 1986, S Korea)

Wheels on Meals (*Kuai can che*) (Sammo Hung Kam-bo, 1984, Hong Kong-Spain)

When Father Was Away on Business (*Otac na sluzbenom putu*) (Emir Kusturica, 1985, Yugoslavia)

Where is the Friend's Home? (*Khane-ye doust kodjast?*) (Abbas Kiarostami, 1987, Iran)

White Badge (*Hayan jeonjaeng*) (Chung Ji-young, 1992, S Korea)

Why Has Bodhi-Dharma Left for the East? (*Dalmaga dongjjogeuro gan kkadalgeun?*) (Bae Yong-kyun, 1989, S Korea)

Wild Animals (*Yasaengdongmul bohoguyeok*) (Kim Ki-duk, 1997, S Korea)

Yesterday (*Yeseuteotei*) (Chong Yunsu, 2002, S Korea)

You My Rose Mellow (*Jeopssikkot dangsin*) (Park Chul-soo, 1988, S Korea)

Young Hero of Shaolin, The (*Chuan ji fang shi yu*) (Ouyang Chun, 1976, Hong Kong/Taiwan)

BIBLIOGRAPHY

Unless otherwise noted, all box office statistics cited in the text are taken from the annual *Korean Cinema Yearbook [Hanguk-yeonghwa-yeon-gam]* published by the Korean Film Council and its predecessor, the Korean Motion Picture Promotion Corporation.

Abelmann, Nancy and Jung-ah Choi (2005) '"Just Because": Comedy, Melodrama and Youth Violence in *Attack the Gas Station*', in Chi-Yun Shin and Julian Stringer (eds) *New Korean Cinema*. Edinburgh: Edinburgh University Press, 132–43.

Anon. (n. d.) 'Fallen Angels', *Variety*. Available at http://www.variety.com/profiles/Film/main/132376/Fallen+Angels.html?dataSet=1&query=Fallen+Angels (accessed 24 October 2009).

____ (1987) 'The vicious cocktail in Chun's tear gas', *Times*, 27 June.

____ (1998) 'Koreans give up their gold to help their country', BBC, 14 January. Available at http://news.bbc.co.uk/2/hi/world/analysis/47496.stm (accessed 24 October 2009).

____ (1999) '98yeonghwa-gye 10dae isyu [Ten issues in the film industry in 1998]', *Cine21*, 183, 26.

____ (2000) '90nyeondae hangungyeonghwa 10dae sageon [Ten events in 1990s Korean cinema]', *Cine21*, 233, 38–41.

____ (2001) *Ensuring Cultural Identity and Diversity in the Era of Globalization*. Seoul: Coalition for Cultural Diversity in Moving Images.

____ (2007) 'DEG Year-End 2006 Home Entertainment Sales Update', *Digital Entertainment Group*. Available at http://www.dvdinformation.com/News/press/CES010807.htm (accessed 24 October 2009).

Bae, Su-gyeong (2005) 'Hanguk-yeonghwa geomyeoljedo-ui byeonhwa [Changes in the censorship system of Korean cinema]', in Kim Dong-ho (ed.) *Hanguk-yeonghwa jeongchaeksa [A History of Korean Film Policy]*. Seoul: Nanam Publishing House, 461–528.

Bak, Hui-seong and Nam Gyeong-hui (2006) *Yeonghwa bunya hallyu hyeonhwang-gwa hwalseonghwa bangan yeongu [Research on the present status and future development plans of film-related hallyu]*. Seoul: Korean Film Council.

Bak, Ji-yeon (2005) 'Yeonghwa-beop jejeong-eseo je 4cha gaejeonggi-kkajiui yeonghwajeongchaek [Film policy from the enactment of the Motion Picture Law to the 4th revision]', in Kim Dong-ho (ed.) *Hanguk-yeonghwa jeongchaeksa [A History of Korean Film Policy]*. Seoul: Nanam Publishing House, 189–267.

Becker, Jasper (1987) 'Rights groups tell of Korean tortures', *Guardian*, 6 June.

Berry, Chris (1999) 'My Queer Korea: Identity, Space, and the 1998 Seoul Queer Film and Video Festival', in *Intersections: Gender, History and Culture in the Asian Context, 2*. Available at http://intersections.anu. edu.au/issue2/Berry.html (accessed 24 October 2009).

____ (2003) '"What's Big About the Big Film?": De-Westernising the Blockbuster in Korea and China', in Julian Stringer (ed.) *Movie Blockbusters*. London: Routledge, 217–29.

Bordwell, David (2007) 'Beyond Asian Minimalism: Hong Sangsoo's Geometry Lesson', in Huh Moonyung (ed.) *Korean Film Directors: Hong Sang-soo*. Seoul: Korean Film Council, 19–29.

Bordwell, David and Kristin Thompson (1997) *Film Art: An Introduction*. Fifth Edition. New York: McGraw-Hill.

Bowyer, Justin (ed.) (2004) *The Cinema of Japan and Korea*. London: Wallflower Press.

Cazzaro, Davide (2005) '"Dovrei Smettere di Mentire": Una Conversazione con Jang Sun-woo', in Davide Cazzaro and Giovanni Spagnoletti (eds) *Il Cinema Sudcoreano Contemporaneo e l'opera di Jang Sun-woo*. Venice: Marsilio Editori, 113–33.

Cazzaro, Davide and Darcy Paquet (2005) 'An interview with Kim Ji-seok', *Koreanfilm.org*. Available at http://www.koreanfilm.org/kimjiseok. html (accessed 24 October 2009).

Cho, Francisca (1999) 'Imagining Nothing and Imaging Otherness in Buddhist Film', in S. Brent Plate and David Jasper (eds) *Imag(in)ing Otherness: Filmic Visions of Living Together*. Atlanta: Scholars, 169–96.

Cho, Hae Joang (2002) '*Sopyonje*: Its Cultural and Historical Meaning', in David E. James and Kyung Hyun Kim (eds) *Im Kwon-Taek: The Making of a Korean National Cinema*. Detroit: Wayne State University Press, 134–56.

Cho, Hae-Joang (2005) 'Reading the "Korean Wave" as a Sign of Global Shift', *Korea Journal*, 45, 4, 147–82.

Choe, Steve (2007) 'Kim Ki-duk's Cinema of Cruelty: Ethics and Spectatorship in the Global Economy', *positions*, 15, 1, 65–90.

Choi, Chungmoo (2002) 'The Politics of Gender, Aestheticism, and Cultural Nationalism in *Sopyonje* and *The Genealogy*', in David E. James and Kyung Hyun Kim (eds) *Im Kwon-Taek: The Making of a Korean National Cinema*. Detroit: Wayne State University Press, 134–56.

Chung, Hye Seung and David Scott Diffrient (2007) 'Forgetting to Remember, Remembering to Forget: The Politics of Memory and Modernity in the Fractured Films of Lee Chang-dong and Hong Sang-soo', in Frances Gateward (ed.) *Seoul Searching: Culture and Identity in Contemporary Korean Cinema*. Albany: State University of New York Press, 115–40.

Chung, Sung-ill (2006) *Korean Film Directors: Im Kwon-taek*. Seoul: Korean Film Council.

Cumings, Bruce (2005) *Korea's Place in the Sun: A Modern History*. Updated Edition. New York: W. W. Norton.

Davis, Darrel William and Emilie Yueh-yu Yeh (2008) *East Asian Screen Industries*. London: British Film Institute.

Eckert, Carter J., Ki-baik Lee, Young Ik Lew, Michael Robinson and Edward W. Wagner (1990) *Korea Old and New: A History*. Cambridge, MA: Korea Institute, Harvard University Press.

Gang, So-won (2005) '1980-nyeondae Hanguk-yeonghwa [1980s Korean Cinema]', in Gina Yu (ed.) *Hanguk-yeonghwa-sa gongbu 1980–1997 [A Study of Korean Film History]*. Seoul: Korean Film Archive, 9–79.

Gateward, Frances (2007) *Seoul Searching: Culture and Identity in Contemporary Korean Cinema*. Albany: State University of New York Press.

Huh, Moonyung (2007a) 'On the Director', in Huh Moonyung (ed.) *Korean Film Directors: Hong Sang-soo*. Seoul: Korean Film Council, 1–15.

____ (2007b) 'Interview', in Huh Moonyung (ed.) *Korean Film Directors: Hong Sang-soo*. Seoul: Korean Film Council, 39–91.

Hwang, Dong-mi (2001) *Hanguk-yeonghwa saneopgujo-bunseok (Analysis of the Structure of the Korean Film Industry)*. Seoul: Korean Film Council.

James, David E. (2002) 'Im Kwon-Taek: Korean National Cinema and Buddhism', in David E. James and Kyung Hyun Kim (eds) *Im Kwon-Taek: The Making of a Korean National Cinema*. Detroit: Wayne State University Press, 47–83.

James, David E. and Kyung Hyun Kim (eds) (2002) *Im Kwon-Taek: The Making of a Korean National Cinema*. Detroit: Wayne State University Press.

Jeong, Jong-hwa (2007) *Hanguk-yeonghwa-sa: Han gwon-euro ingneun yeonghwa 100-nyeon [Korean Film History: 100 Years of Film in One Volume]*. Seoul: Korean Film Archive.

Jo, Jun-hyeong (2005) 'Hanguk-yeonghwa-saneop-gwa Jeongchaek [Korean Film Industry and Policy]', in Gina Yu (ed.) *Hanguk-yeonghwa-sa gongbu 1980–1997 [A Study of Korean Film History 1980–1997]*. Seoul: Korean Film Archive, 143–205.

Kim, Hak-su (2002) *Seukeurin bakkui hanguk-yeonghwa-sa [Korean Film History Outside the Screen]*. Seoul: Inmul-gwa Sasangsa.

Kim, Hyung-seok (2008) *Korean Film Directors: Kim Jee-woon*. Seoul: Korean Film Council.

Kim, Kyung Hyun (2002) 'Korean cinema and Im Kwon-Taek', in David James and Kyung Hyun Kim (eds) *Im Kwon-Taek: The Making of a Korean National Cinema*. Detroit: Wayne State University Press, 19–46.

____ (2004) *The Remasculinization of Korean Cinema*. Durham, NC: Duke University Press.

Kim, Mee hyun (ed.) (2007) *Korean Cinema: From Origins to Renaissance*. Seoul: Communication Books.

Kim, Samuel S. (2000) 'Korea and Globalization (Segyehwa): A Framework for Analysis', in Samuel S. Kim (ed.) *Korea's Globalization*. Cambridge: Cambridge University Press, 1–28.

Kim, So-hui (2004) 'Editorial: Well-made', *Cine21*, 436, 16.

Kim, Soyoung (2005) '"Cine-Mania" or Cinephilia: Film Festivals and the Identity Question', in Chi-Yun Shin and Julian Stringer (eds) *New Korean Cinema*. Edinburgh: Edinburgh University Press, 79– 91.

Kim, Sunah (2007a) '*Jangsangotmae* and the Struggle to Screen *Night Before the Strike*', in Kim Mee hyun (ed.) *Korean Cinema: From Origins to Renaissance*. Seoul: Communication Books, 331–2.

____ (2007b) '*Sopyonje* and the Revival of Nationalism', in Kim Mee hyun (ed.) *Korean Cinema: From Origins to Renaissance*. Seoul: Communication Book , 339–41.

Kim, Young-jin (2007a) *Korean Film Directors: Lee Chang-dong*. Seoul: Korean Film Council.

____ (2007b) *Korean Film Directors: Park Chan-wook*. Seoul: Korean Film Council.

Korea Motion Picture Promotion Corporation (1980–99) *Hanguk-yeonghwa-yeongam* [*Korean Cinema Yearbook*]. Seoul: Jimmundang.

Korean Film Council (2000–07) *Hanguk-yeonghwa-yeongam* [*Korean Cinema Yearbook*]. Seoul: Communication Books.

Lagandré, Cédric (2006) 'Spoken Words in Suspense', in Adrien Gombeaud, Anaïd Demir, Cédric Lagandré, Catherine Capdeville-Zeng and Daniele Rivière, *Kim Ki-duk*. Paris: Dis Voir, 59–93.

Lee, Hae-jin (2001) *Kim Ki-duk, From Crocodile to Address Unknown*. Seoul: LJ Film.

Lee, Hyangjin (2000) *Contemporary Korean Cinema: Identity, Culture, Politics*. Manchester: Manchester University Press.

Lee, Hyeong-gi (1989) 'UIP-jikbae galdeung galsurok simgak [Discord over UIP direct distribution grows ever more serious]', *Hankook Ilbo*, 31 August, 9.

Lee, Keeheyung (2005) 'Morae sigye: "Social Melodrama" and the Politics of Memory in Contemporary South Korea', in Kathleen McHugh and Nancy Abelmann (eds) *South Korean Golden Age Melodrama: Gender, Genre, and National Cinema*. Detroit: Wayne State University Press, 229–45.

Lee, Yeon-ung (1989) 'Mijikbae yeonghwa-gwan-6got yeonsoe-piseup [Series of attacks on six movie theatres screening directly distributed American films]', *Segye Ilbo*, 15 August, 14.

Nam, Dong-cheol (1997) '98nyeon, migungeseo gilchanneun hanhae [98, A Year of Searching for a Road out of the Labyrinth]', *Cine21*, 132, 24–5.

Oberdorfer, Don (2001) *The Two Koreas: A Contemporary History*. New York: Basic Books.

Paquet, Darcy (2003) 'An interview with E J-yong', *Koreanfilm.org*. Available at http://www.koreanfilm.org/ejyong.html (accessed 24 October 2009).

____ (2005) 'The Korean Film Industry: 1992 to the Present', in Chi-Yun Shin and Julian Stringer (eds) *New Korean Cinema*. Edinburgh: Edinburgh University Press, 32–50.

____ (2007a) 'Higher risks don't curb Korean cash flow', *Variety*, 12 March, A1.

____ (2007b) '"Host" conquers fears, scares up profits', *Variety*, 12 March, A6.

____ (2007c) '*Christmas in August* and Korean Melodrama', in Frances Gateward (ed.) *Seoul Searching: Culture and Identity in Contemporary Korean Cinema*. Albany: State University of New York Press, 37–54.

____ (2009) 'Market swings: Stock-market listings and the Korean film industry', *Journal of Japanese and Korean Cinema*, 1, 1, 83–91.

Park, Daniel D. H. (ed.) (2008) *Korean Film Database Book 1995–2008*. Seoul: Korean Film Council.

Park, Nohchool (2009) 'The new waves at the margin: an historical overview of South Korean cinema movements 1975–84', *Journal of Japanese and Korean Cinema*, 1, 1, 45–63.

Park, Seung Hyun (2002) 'Film Censorship and Political Legitimation in South Korea, 1987–1992', *Cinema Journal*, 42, 1, 120–38.

Rayns, Tony (1996) 'Seoul Notes: Comings and Goings', *Sight and Sound*, September, 5.

____ (2007) *Korean Film Directors: Jang Sun-woo*. Seoul: Korean Film Council.

Robinson, Michael (2005) 'Contemporary Cultural Production in South Korea: Vanishing Meta-Narratives of Nation', in Chi-Yun Shin and Julian Stringer (eds) *New Korean Cinema*. Edinburgh: Edinburgh University Press, 15–31.

____ (2007) *Korea's Twentieth Century Odyssey: A Short History*. Honolulu: University of Hawaii Press.

Russell, Mark James (2008) *Pop Goes Korea: Behind the Revolution in Movies, Music, and Internet Culture*. Berkeley: Stone Bridge Press.

Shim, Doobo (2006) 'Hybridity and the rise of Korean popular culture in Asia', *Media, Culture & Society*, 28, 1, 25–44.

Shin, Chi-Yun and Julian Stringer (eds) (2005) *New Korean Cinema*. Edinburgh: Edinburgh University Press.

Shin, Jeeyoung (2005) 'Globalization and New Korean Cinema', in Chi-Yun Shin and Julian Stringer (eds) *New Korean Cinema*. Edinburgh: Edinburgh University Press, 51–62.

Standish, Isolde (1994) 'Korean Cinema and the New Realism: Text and Context', in Wimal Dissanayake (ed.) *Colonialism and Nationalism in Asian Cinema*. Bloomington: Indiana University Press, 65–89.

Stringer, Julian (2003) 'Introduction', in Julian Stringer (ed.) *Movie Blockbusters*. London: Routledge, 1–14.

Swain, Jon (1987) 'Koreans braced for brutal backlash: Americans are warned to lie low', *Times*, 21 June.

Tram, Mark and Jasper Becker (1987) 'US tells Seoul not to impose martial law', *Guardian*, 22 June.

Watts, David (1987) 'Police take a beating in Korean violence', *Times*, 19 June.

Yecies, Brian (2007) 'Parleying Culture against Trade: Hollywood's Affairs with Korea's Screen Quotas', *Korea Observer*, 38, 1, 1–32.

Yi, Hyeok-sang (2005) 'Hanguk-yeonghwa jinheung-gigu-ui yeoksa [A history of Korean film promotion organisations]', in Kim Dong-ho (ed.), *Hanguk-yeonghwa jeongchaeksa [A History of Korean Film Policy]*. Seoul: Nanam Publishing House, 351–460.

Yoo, Boo-woong (1988) *Korean Pentacostalism: Its History and Theology*. New York: Verlag Peter Lang.

INDEX

Milton Keynes UK
Ingram Content Group UK Ltd.
UKHW041039110224
437582UK00005B/367

9 781906 660253